Re-Incarceration

A True Story of Life Inside the Revolving Door of Jail.

By

Tyke McCarthy

"The Best Training a First-Time Writer Could Have Is a Troubled Childhood."

-Ernest Hemingway

"A Little Jail Time Never Hurt Anyone. It's A Lot of Jail Time That Hurts."

-John Dillinger

I would like to dedicate the book to Reba. She has been nothing short of an angel from heaven. Life has tossed us a hand full of obstacles, but with Reba by my side, we tackle every problem one at a time.

Table of Contents

CHAPTER 1

The Beginning

"The Revolving Door" – most humans picture this term as an entrance to a large downtown office building or a grand hotel. In my world, it's known as the pathetic existence of the repeat criminal offender: drug dealers, crooks, and armed robbers who are unsuccessful at what they do. I am all of the above. As a result, out of my sixty-three years on this planet, I've spent over half of those years in jail. My name is Michael Harry McCarthy. Most people know me as Tyke. My story is true; my arrest record and criminal history are all a matter of public record. How I'm not doing a life sentence right now is one of many miracles in my life.

My story of re-incarceration begins in the third grade. I was eight years old, and I got pinched for shoplifting from the local grocery market. I was busted with candy, toys, and a Playboy magazine – all the must-haves for an eight-year-old boy. Given the title of the book and an arrest record that starts at eight, you may picture my background and upbringing as less than fortunate, but that couldn't be further from the truth. I was born on February 9, 1959, in San Francisco, California, into a loving Irish Catholic family. I have four brothers and one sister. We were raised in the upper-middle-class neighborhoods of Marin, California. I'll refer back to my family as the story continues, but one thing is for certain: in my family, I was and always will be the jet-black sheep.

There's a familiar saying, "Although you may choose your friends, you can't choose your family." But I would choose my family, no question! I grew up with a passion for three things: baseball, motorcycles, and motorcycle chicks. My next encounter with the authorities didn't come until after my twelfth birthday. It was also the twelfth year of my birth that I had my first sighting of a group of Hell's Angels motorcycle riders in Oakland, California, flying down Highway 580. We were traveling in the family station wagon, visiting relatives in the San Leandro area, and that was it; I was hooked. I had no idea what type of motorcycles they were riding, but that was it for me. From then on, I would be a motorcycle enthusiast.

My first motorized bike was a minibike I bought in the Sunset District of San Francisco. I was twelve years old, and this first motorbike was also my next police encounter since the shoplifting pinch four years earlier. I took the bus to San Francisco with sixty dollars I had scraped together. I had seen the advertisement in the newspaper for a three-and-a-half-horsepower Briggs and Stratton minibike. I called the number listed and arranged the purchase. I didn't care how I was going to get it home or how I would get my parents to let me keep it – it just didn't matter. I hadn't even laid eyes on it; I just knew that I wanted it. I bought it from a teenager dressed in disco clothes. I remember thinking how stupid he looked. Those thoughts quickly passed as I headed north on Nineteenth Avenue on my first motorbike at the top speed of thirty miles per hour. I stopped for gas just before Golden Gate Park. I filled the gas tank up for eighty-five cents, headed down Park Presidio Avenue, and made my way through the McArthur Tunnel. You should have seen the looks I was getting from the people passing by me.

I made it safely down to Doyle Drive and up to the northbound Highway 101 toll plaza of the Golden Gate Bridge. My plan was to take the sidewalk across the bridge to get back to Marin County, but right at the entrance to the sidewalk, by the Roundhouse souvenir shop, stood three cops on foot – just my luck. I stayed on the street and ran to the toll booth plaza; back then, you had to pay a toll both north and southbound. I had put the last of my cash inside the gas tank anyway. As I made my way onto the slow lane of the bridge, I could hear all three cops yelling at me. I tucked in low, like a superbike racer, and grabbed a handful of throttle. I made it across the bridge in what seemed like a friggin' hour. At the time, I didn't care. I was in the wind, blasting across the Golden Gate Bridge. The goosebumps I was experiencing were intoxicating. I got past the Vista Point exit and was headed for the Sausalito exit when, out of nowhere, two California Highway Patrol cars were behind me with red lights and sirens. I must have looked like I wasn't going to pull over because the squad car, right behind me, swooped up on my left side and ran me into the dirt embankment of the Sausalito exit's shoulder. Curses! They had me.

These two John Wayne-looking highway cops were actually good ol' boys. They said I may have been the only person to ride a minibike across the Golden Gate Bridge. At the time, it didn't mean much; I was just trying to make my way home on my new bike. Well, even though these highway cops got a big kick out of me, it didn't stop them from impounding my minibike and giving me a ticket. I suppose I was lucky not to be on my way to juvenile hall, but I was heartbroken over my minibike. For years, I never told my parents about that ticket or what I did. I just threw the ticket away and kept my mouth shut. I never saw the minibike again, but I was even more hooked on motorcycles. My next motorcycle came to me a couple of years later. I was fourteen years old. It was a Suzuki 125. I bought it for one hundred dollars from an old hippy-type guy in the town of Forest Knolls in western Marin County.

I had been having run-ins with the law on a regular basis over petty things like breaking curfew, disturbing the peace, and vandalism – nothing to brag about, just juvenile delinquent stuff. My Suzuki and I would soon be in a chase with the police that brought a lot of attention. I had the motorcycle for over a month now, and I was illegally riding it everywhere. I'd ride it to junior high school and let the chicks check me out, but I wouldn't attend class. I guess I was too cool for school. Anyway, a group of "no goods" and I were drinking and partying late at night down at the neighborhood creek, and the noise we were making attracted the police. In no time, we were all making a run for it. I got my bike started and made it to the street. With a top speed of maybe forty to forty-five miles per hour, I was no match for the police cruisers in a high-speed chase, but with the advantage of front lawns, alleyways, and doubling back every time a squad car got too close, I soon had five or six squad cars going crazy – sirens and lights flashing late into the night. The chase went on for over an hour, with me stopping in shadowy, hidden areas a couple of times and then making another break for it, but one patrolman had enough. He made it up to my left side and squeezed me into a line of parked cars. I was arrested and booked into juvenile hall in Lucas Valley, California. My father came and got me out the next day. I was playing center field for an all-star team that was doing pretty well, and it was game day. In my family, baseball was huge. All my brothers played well, and my father played for the San Francisco Seals. Both my father and the authorities warned me about my motorcycle lawlessness, but my motorcycle appetite grew stronger. The news of the motorcycle chase traveled and got the attention of a local biker named Bob. Bob was a few years older than me, but one hour after we met, we were best bros, and that friendship continues today. Bob seemed to have it all: a badass Harley shovelhead, an antique hot rod pick-up, and an unsatisfying appetite for the motorcycle lifestyle. Bob's family and mine were well acquainted; he attended school with my brother, and our fathers played golf together. Bob ran with an older crowd, and they all went on bike runs together. I didn't own a Harley, much less a driver's license, but that would all change – the part about owning a Harley, anyway. The driver's license would not come for years later, but this was no matter – first things first. By this time, I was fifteen years old and a freshman at Terra Linda High School in the city of San Rafael, California.

CHAPTER 2

No Turning Back

The year was 1974, and an old hoodlum friend of mine had just been released from the California Youth Authority. This was a state-run lock-up for juvenile offenders, also known as a state prison for underage hoods. My friend's name was Foud. The statute of limitations has run out on all of these crimes I'll be sharing in this story, but I don't see the point of using real names other than my own. Even though my complete criminal history is a matter of public record, there are a few real names I could use to further the authenticity of my story: Sheriff Charles T. Prandi, Sgt. Skip Richardson, San Rafael police Sgt. Mike Kelly and I can't forget Marin County District Attorney Kit Mitchell. These lifelong Marin County authority members knew me well.

Anyway, with my friend Foud out on state parole, 1974 became the year of "no turning back" on a life of serious criminal activity that would last for thirty-five years. It was also the year we planned, executed, and got away with armed bank robbery. At seventeen years old, I believe that Foud saw this crime as a way to fame and fortune. At fifteen years old, I saw it as a quick way to owning a Chopper motorcycle. Either way, this is what happened in the spring of 1974.

Foud and I were spending time together partying down at Miller Creek in a small community named Marinwood. Foud's family home was right behind mine in Marinwood. The bank heist idea was first hatched from watching too many re-runs of "The Untouchables". At first, it was something we joked about sarcastically, but it grew more serious as we continued getting away with petty heists around town. I suppose our empty heads were gathering up courage with the ability to be successful at petty crime. Why shouldn't we move up the larceny ladder? The bank we had in mind was one town over. We went to case the bank a week before the robbery. I couldn't believe we were actually going to go through with it, and casing a bank seemed silly since I didn't know what to look for. I let Foud do all the planning thus far. I just liked the idea of going by the bank because right next to the bank was a group of stores where all the pretty girls hung out.

The day the bank heist was planned for became tomorrow. I remember I was playing centerfield for Terra Linda High School the night before the robbery, and I can still remember thinking to myself about the next day and the robbery, saying to myself, out in the centerfield, "No way this shit is gonna happen."

The next day showed up, and I found myself wearing two sets of clothes. I had a mask, gloves, and a pistol in my pockets as I rode the bus to the next town, sitting next to Foud. I'm pretty sure I was in a mild state of shock that we had gotten this far. The bank itself was a three-story structure, with the first floor being a parking garage. There were two entrances to the bank. One was a two-story staircase outside that led up to the west entrance of the bank and an elevator directly under the middle of the building, going from the garage floor to a lobby inside the bank building. This is where Foud and I now stood shoulder to shoulder, waiting for the elevator car to descend to the garage floor. We were wearing ski masks and gloves when the elevator car rang its arrival at the garage floor. We heard voices inside the elevator car. We quickly turned, taking one step each, and bounced off each other. We turned quickly again and were able to dart behind opposite cars undetected.

Four or five people exited the elevator. They left the garage in several cars, and once again, Foud and I were facing the elevator, waiting for its arrival. The time was 4:15 pm, and we worried more employees might be leaving the building. We listened for voices as the elevator car arrived. No voices and my heart was pounding at a very dangerous rate. The elevator doors opened, and no one was inside. We moved inside the car, and Foud pushed the second-floor button. The doors closed. I could hear my heart beating inside my chest over the elevator music. As the elevator began to lift us to the second floor, I could tell I was sweating like no other time in my life inside the two layers of clothing I had on. The elevator stopped at the second floor with another deafening ring. With masks and gloves on, both of us armed, the elevator doors began to open. Not knowing what was waiting for us in the lobby, as the doors continued to open, my heart was going like a poker card in a child's bicycle spokes. No one was in the lobby to greet us. We peeked out into the lobby in both directions. There were several offices to the left of the lobby, and to the right, there were two big glass doors leading to the inside of the bank. We started to slowly emerge from the elevator, and the doors started to close and squirted us both out into the open exposure of the lobby. We made our way to the double glass doors leading into the bank undetected. The business part of the bank was out of sight from the glass doors.

At this point, with masks on and guns drawn, we were committed. I looked at Foud one last time, and he looked ill. I asked Foud, "Ready?" He shook his head yes. Knowing my life would never be the same and terrified, we exploded into the bank, yelling, "Robbery, everyone down!" Foud went for the bank's counter. I covered the people on the floor with a .22 caliber pistol with no bullets. Foud, with all his little league ability, leaped the counter and started rifling the cash drawers. I eyeballed the west side of the bank where we planned to exit down the outside staircase. Our plan was no more than ninety seconds inside the bank. We got that from an old episode of "The Untouchables." As Foud gathered up the loot, I had no idea how much time we had been inside the bank, so I just yelled, "Time!" Foud popped up from behind the counter, jumped up over one of the bank teller's windows, and made his way over to me. We exited the bank's west side without a word. We cleared both flights of stairs in mid-air, made it to the parking garage level, and then sprinted the fifty yards across the parking lot to a medical building next to the bank that had an underground garage. We quickly peeled off our top layer of clothing, threw them inside some trash cans, put our gloves, masks, and pistols inside the money bag, and emerged out the other end of the medical building, all the while hearing the sirens of closing police cars. A couple of police cars even roared right past us, making their way to the bank.

We made our way to an abandoned lot on the side of a nearby hill. From where we hid, we could see and hear the commotion going on in the bank's parking lot. I could have thrown a baseball and hit the police cars. We were still that close. So, what did we do with all this going on in our eyes and ears? We counted the loot. We stuffed the cash in our pockets along with the pistols and tried to figure out how to get home. We hadn't got this far in the planning. It was maybe 5:30 pm by now, and the cover of darkness was with us. We made our way back to the little strip mall where all the local hoods and pretty girls hung out. The very minute we emerged into the light and exposure of the strip mall, the first sight we encountered was a police cruiser slowly driving through the mall with the cruiser's driver's side window down, and the officer driving was staring straight at the two of us. He had the police radio mic up to his mouth. He slowed down even more. I didn't know what the words "internally combust" meant, but I knew what it felt like. The police cruiser kept going, but all the time, the officer was eyeing us down, and Foud and I were standing there with all our pockets stuffed with the bank loot and pistols. We saw a couple of hoods we knew with a car and got a ride back to Marinwood. The next day, the heist was all over the news. We cleared just about five thousand in the bank heist, but the news had the robbery's take at over ten thousand, and I realized Foud and I weren't the only crooks that day. I was pretty nervous for a few days, but bombing around town on my new Chopper motorcycle seemed to ease my nerves a bit.

The few people who knew what Foud and I had done were too scared to talk about it, but that wouldn't last with what happened next. I was spending more time with Bob and the motorcycle crew he ran with. Although I wasn't yet the owner of a Harley, I seemed, to them anyway, to be on the right track. I was still in school and running around on my motorcycle every night. The bank loot soon ran dry, and I found myself back in the company of Foud. The movie "Easy Rider" had just come out and was breaking box office records all over. It was set to open at the Highway 101 drive-in theatre in two days. We both knew the layout of the drive-in theatre. It was one exit south of our hometown of Marinwood at the Lucas Valley exit off Highway 101. We had walked there many nights and sat off to the east side, where there was an old auto-wrecking yard. We would watch the movies for free, sitting in busted-up auto chairs.

The next two days before the movie opened at the drive-in were spent planning the robbery of the theatre. Directly across the street from the theatre was a small bluegill pond where we used to fish, which provided plenty of cover for my motorcycle and our approach to the heist. The plan wasn't complicated: wait until the place was full of cars, let the movie start playing for a few minutes, and then rob the ticket booth. Right off the bat, we screwed up. We got there a bit too early and mulled around way too much, trying to recon the ticket booth. We were seen by an employee of the drive-in who we knew from high school. So, with all our wisdom, bank robbery background, and "Untouchables" re-runs, we robbed the ticket booth anyway. We made our escape on my motorcycle and got back to Marinwood safely, or so we thought. A half-hour after the robbery, we parked at one of the two gas stations in downtown Marinwood, sitting on a small bR-Rick wall right beside a couple of phone booths, waiting for some hoods to call us back and let us know where everyone was partying that night. Two Marin County sheriff's cars pulled up and, without any hesitation, jumped out of their patrol cars with guns drawn, yelling at the two of us to get face down on the ground. Our description and the possibility of a getaway on a motorcycle were all over the police radio. In no time, we had ten cop cars surrounding us and my motorcycle.

When the first two sheriffs showed up, quickly stopping right in front of where we sat on that R-Rick wall, both Foud and I emptied our pockets of the stolen robbery loot and dropped it all in the bushes behind the wall. Foud also dropped the pistol with his take of the loot. After we were handcuffed and shoved into the back of a patrol car, the officers quickly found the stolen loot and pistol, further sealing our fate. We were both booked into Marin County juvenile hall for armed robbery. I had just come off a baseball season that might have shown the possibility of a career in baseball for me or at least a scholarship to a good school. My father, bless his heart, hired a well-known attorney named Bill Wiesich. Mr. Wiesich was formerly a District Attorney before going into private practice. My father knew Bill personally from his years in law enforcement with the federal government. I didn't know it at the time, but things were about to get worse. With the publicity we received from the movie theatre robbery and the rumors flying around about how Foud and I had also taken down a bank a few months back, the FBI came and pulled us out of the juvenile hall and busted our balls for hours inside the intimidating interview rooms of the federal building. We lawyered up; believe it or not, we got that from "The Untouchables" too. It friggin' worked, and the frustrated feds brought us back to juvenile hall, although I was positive, I hadn't seen the last of them. When my father got word of this, the look he gave me said, "Fuck me. What have I raised here in this kid?"

Two weeks later, we were in juvenile court, setting a date for trial on our armed robbery charge. Our judge, a man who had been sitting on the juvenile judge's bench for years, did not like me and Foud right from the first day of our court proceedings. He had already sent Foud to the California Youth Authority two years prior, and with the serious charge of armed robbery we were facing, we found out later that this judge had seen surveillance photos of the bank robbery and was convinced we were guilty of it. He ruled to move our trial to the county courthouse since, as he explained, it has the county jail there, and that's where these two hoods belong. His name was Judge Blane. My attorney objected to his remarks, citing "prejudice," but back then, in 1974, there was no such thing.

We went to trial at the Marin County Civic Center two months later. My attorney Bill Wiesich, his associate Randy Highbach, Foud, Foud's court-appointed attorney, and I. The District Attorney marched in the reluctant high school student who put us in the area of the robbery and the arresting officers who found the money and pistol. Old Judge Blane took just ten minutes to sustain the petition, which meant he found us guilty. In juvenile court trials, there's no jury, just the judge. Judge Jack Blaine sent Foud back to the California Youth Authority, and with me, he was a bit more sympathetic, but I soon changed all that. He sent me to a series of lock-up facilities that offered counseling for troubled youths. I bucked the system the whole way. I was sent back to juvenile hall, where I promptly escaped with no other plan than to party. After about two weeks on the run from the authorities, I was arrested in a stolen car. I attempted to reach my attorney by telephone from juvenile hall, but Bill was murdered a week earlier by an out-on-parole disgruntled ex-convict from Bill's past as a D.A. Damn shame. Bill Wiesich was good people. His associate Randy Highbach went on to become a Marin County Court judge. With not much help in my legal situation, I pled guilty to car theft and escape and was sentenced to one year in the California Youth Authority. I was considered a good dude at Marin County juvenile hall, so when the time came to chain me up and transport me to the Youth Authority, the two juvenile hall cops were cool as shit. What I mean by that is right when we cleared the juvenile hall property, the two cops started lighting up a few marijuana doobies. By the time I got to the state facility in Sacramento, I was sixteen years old and tripping big time! I said goodbye to the cool cops, and some real ball-busters took custody of me. I spent a year in a facility outside of Stockton, California called Karl Holton—named after some warden.

CHAPTER 3

Baseball, Love, and a Life of Crime

I paroled from the California Youth Authority at the age of seventeen, the first of many paroles at that age. I'll explain a little later what I mean by that. I enrolled back at Terra Linda High School for my senior year. However, my grades quickly slipped because I preferred hanging out in front of the school and smoking pot with the local hoods. I was transferred to a "continuation" school until the semester break, then readmitted to Terra Linda High because the baseball season was about to begin, and I was needed in the outfield. It seems baseball was the only thing I was good at that wasn't against the law. These days, I wish I had been more serious about the game back then. But at that time in my life, I wasn't hungry for anything but trouble. I couldn't even appreciate the gift of being allowed back to my high school to play ball without causing some trouble. Four days before the opening game, two other players and I were caught smoking pot in front of the school. Two of us were suspended for three games, while the other player, who was going to be cut anyway, was removed from the team. We lost the home opener, so the suspension was lifted, and the other player and I started every game for the rest of the season. I love baseball and still play today, although mostly with the "penal leagues."

Anyway, it was during these high school years that I met the love of my life. We'll call her "Dish" because that's what she was—a Dish! My love for her continues to this day. But this is no love story. After high school, I went through one lousy job after another until I found real employment in the form of jewelry theft. It began small but quickly blossomed into a full-time endeavor. The price of gold and silver was constantly rising in the late seventies and early eighties, and I took full advantage. With more and more money coming in, I was in a constant state of partying. Every day felt like Saturday.

Back in those days, jewelry stores would naively leave most of their jewelry in the display cases overnight, believing their alarm systems provided sufficient security. I would scout for a jewelry store, conducting recon and research missions from afar using binoculars or a small telescope. I would watch the employees lock up for the night and exit the store. I would then enter using various methods, always with the same smash-and-grab game plan. I was no electrician, so bypassing the alarm system was out of the question. My one-man crime wave was relentless, and word got around to the jewelry store companies. As a result, they began locking up their merchandise in safes overnight. I had pulled off countless smash-and-grabs, but this safe twist was not going to stop me. I began conducting my recon from inside the jewelry stores, observing the size of the safes and whether or not I could remove them quickly enough to beat the police response to the alarm.

I had devised a method for opening safes. I would use a drill press to drill a series of holes in a large circle, then drill more holes in between to create one large round hole in the side of the safe. It required a lot of drill bits and about a quart of oil, but I managed to open many safes this way. Safe cracking was time-consuming, but I got into every safe I stole. I was a 20th-century pirate—or a friggin' prick—whatever, as long as it was Saturday night again, and I could party on!

One such safe I stole was from a privately-owned gas station in the North Bay area. Back in the early eighties, there were many gas stations that dealt only in cash. This robbery turned into a heart attack waiting to happen. I was getting gas in an old GMC pick-up I owned and noticed an employee counting cash at the desk through the station's office window. As I finished pumping gas into my truck, I walked towards the office to pay. I was more than half-tempted to pull out the .38-caliber pistol I had on me instead of my wallet. But as I got closer to the office, I saw the employee putting the bundles of cash inside a safe. The safe was about four feet high and two feet in diameter. I quickly abandoned my armed robbery urge and conducted a quick recon of the inside of the gas station's office. All windows and doors were wired with alarms, but the two-bay garage part of the station was not open for business. The gas station was only open for the retail sale of gasoline. The garage bays were closed off with ¾' sheets of plywood. No alarm was present except for the office where the safe was kept.

Although the garage was closed, plenty of tools remained inside. I scanned the inside of the garage, noting everything I would need for that night's robbery. I walked back to my truck and spent the next hour planning my heist. Around 11:30 pm that night, I parked my pick-up in a bowling alley parking lot directly behind the gas station. I made my way through a weed-covered field that separated the parking lot from the back of the gas station. According to the sign on the office door, it was two hours after closing, and a quick peek through the office side window confirmed no one was working late. My safe was right where I left it. I easily pried loose one of the ¾' sheets of plywood covering the entrance to one of the garage bays using my truck's tire iron. The plywood was heavy, at least fourteen feet high and four feet wide. I slipped into the garage and leaned the plywood back in place to look good for anyone passing by.

I pulled on my ski mask and gloves and grabbed a sledgehammer I had spotted earlier that day. With only the doors and windows alarmed, I used the sledgehammer to make my own door through the flimsy wall in no time. But when I got my hands on the safe, I realized it was incredibly heavy! I went back through the hole I made in the wall and grabbed a floor jack on wheels from the garage. I brought it into the office, wheeled it next to the safe, and tipped the safe over, landing it on its side right on top of the floor jack. I turned the floor jack around using the handle and pivoting the safe on the floor jack's wheels. Then I pushed the whole thing as fast as I could towards the hole in the wall, and the safe slid right through, slamming onto the garage floor. Just then, I was hit with a car's headlights as it pulled into the gas station. I hit the floor hard. I knew I hadn't been seen by whoever was driving because the car slowly cruised around the back of the station before making its way out front. When the car was around back, I moved fast and low out of the office back into the garage where the safe had landed.

I looked at the sheet of plywood where I first made my entrance. With the wind picking up, the plywood was moving around a bit. I ran low again to hold the plywood in place. Damn the luck. The car stopped right in front of me and the large sheet of plywood. I didn't know who or what was in the vehicle, but I quickly got my answer when I heard the bone-chilling squelch of the police radio. The wind picked up, and here I was, holding this large sheet of plywood with all my strength, so close to this cop that I could hear his conversations on the radio. He was dealing with some paperwork that lasted about forty-five minutes but seemed much longer before he received a disturbance call and sped off.

I eased up on my hold of the plywood, and sure enough, it would have fallen if I hadn't been holding it in place. I pulled back the bottom of the plywood another three feet and leaned it once again against its frame. This way, it had more of a lean-to help it stay in place. I hurried back through the hole I made in the wall, grabbed the floor jack, and brought it back into the garage. I stretched the stiffness out of my bones from holding the plywood against the breezy night for an hour, motivated by the desire not to be fitted with handcuffs. I once again tilted the safe onto the floor jack and carefully wheeled it out the way I had come in over two hours earlier. I slowly wheeled it to the back of the station, where there was a two-foot drop-off from the pavement into the weed-covered field. I stopped at the edge of the drop-off, ran over to the bowling alley parking lot, and fired up my truck. I bounced my truck through the field and backed it up to the drop-off, where the safe waited. I ran around to the back of the truck, dropped the tailgate, jacked up the floor jack as high as it would go, and managed to slide the safe into the back of the truck.

The weight of the safe seriously messed up my vehicle's handling and the getaway. I slowly drove to my buddy's house (I had no choice!), who had a machine shop and drill press. I backed the truck up to the entrance of his shop, and with the tailgate down, I got going about twenty-five miles per hour and slammed on the brakes, and the safe slid out the back of my truck, completing a perfect 1 1/2 dive before landing right in front of my buddy's shop. We maneuvered the safe over to the drill press and immediately started drilling a series of holes in a circle about ten inches wide. We also did my classic move of drilling holes between the holes. It took about four hours before I was handing out a cut to my buddy and peeling out with over twelve thousand dollars for my trouble. The year was 1978. I met up with another career man that I first became acquainted with inside the juvenile hall. We'll call him Bowl. Bowl was just as dedicated to the pursuit of precious metals as I was. We teamed up for a while and began a journey that would rival many famous crime sprees.

CHAPTER 4

Burglar's Logic

Now, personally, I've always considered burglary a spineless act of a crime. Considering my background, it would be hard for me to convince anyone of these feelings. I can't speak for anyone else on this subject, but that's how I feel. But for me, when I would get involved in such a crime, it was always the rich, well-insured, and well-to-do. With every large estate I robbed, the owners would always claim to the authorities and their insurance companies at least twice the amount that actually was stolen. In my twisted way of thinking, throughout these years, the robbed would make money on their exaggerated (fraudulent) claims to the insurance companies, the alarm companies would be hired to install better alarm systems, the cops' job security would be guaranteed, and the insurance companies would offset their losses by raising premiums. I, or so I thought, was busy stimulating the local economy. Over the years, Bowl and I robbed hundreds of such estates either together or separately in between prison terms, of course!

We hit a plush pad the same day we teamed up in 1978. My game plan always stayed the same when alarm systems were involved: smash, grab, and have a good escape route. However, Bowl added some variety to the plan by having some skills with electronics. He had already been to state prison on a two-year stretch, where he acquired his knowledge. What a world. Go to prison for an illegal act and learn a whole new skill set for beating a burglar alarm. Who said that crime doesn't pay? Anyway, Bowl didn't know as much as he led on. More than once, I had to run for my life after relying on Bowl's electronic skills. He did get us past this first estate's alarm.

We were in the town of Tiburon, California. We parked my truck at a local motel parking lot and got out wearing jogging clothes with burglary tools taped to the inside of our pulled-up socks. We jogged to an adjacent community named Belvedere Island. There's lots of money on Belvedere Island. It would not be my last visit. Dusk was upon us as we jogged through this very exclusive neighborhood. We came across a beautiful three-story estate with all the signs telling crooks like us, "No one is here. Rob me." We stopped our run and went in for a closer reconnaissance. The place was absolutely jaw-droppingly gorgeous, with a breathtaking San Francisco skyline view. From what I could see, the place was well-armed but screaming out to be pinched. All signs point to yes when you see a paper in the driveway and a mailbox full of mail, but there's the active alarm system to take into account.

We went to work. Bowl had me help him to the roof. He said this particular alarm system went out over the phone lines. As it turned out, he was right. He whispered down from the roof that he had cut the phone lines. I easily pried open the palace's back sliding glass doors. We were in. I didn't stop stressing during the entire heist. I couldn't stop thinking that maybe Bowl was wrong. We were inside this estate for over thirty minutes. We had found a wall safe that we weren't leaving without. We found a sledgehammer and a double-bit ax from the garage, and we attacked the safe like madmen. When we were getting tools out of the garage, we came across a new four-door Jaguar, and, as it happened, the keys to it were hanging from a hook right next to the garage entrance.

The wall safe was located behind a mirror that Bowl found while I was bagging up the jewelry box's contents. That safe was a bitch to get loose. We damn near had to take the wall out with it. The safe had two large steel rods sticking out of both sides, which secured it to wall studs. Fifteen minutes of Bowl and me beating the wall into confetti, and we were loading our score into the Jag. Bowl jumped into the driver's seat. The jewelry box and I rode shotgun. Bowl hit the button for the garage's automatic remote control, and we backed out of that felony. I was dropped at the truck and followed Bowl all the way to my buddy's machine shop. Three hours later, we were dividing up five thousand in cash. We got over seven thousand for the contents of the jewelry box, and my machine shop buddy took the new Jag for his cut.

Bowl and I would also dabble a bit in robbing drug dealers of their products. This was a touchy hobby, even though the police were rarely involved. You had to be on your toes about "rats" and "revenge." Most drug dealers are cowards, but by being the person that holds what a lot of people want, they develop false feelings of courage from everyone kissing their asses all day. Just to get a taste of what they have, the rats that they would pay to find out who robbed them would usually just make up shit to be rewarded with a taste of dope. It was no big secret that Bowl and I were very active in the business of robbing drug dealers. So, our names were dropped by such rats. As a result, we were blamed for a lot of shit we didn't do.

Now, the revenge part would start, and like I said, most drug dealers are cowards. They would pay someone to move on us, who were usually some other crooks that were friends of ours, and they would take the drug dealers' revenge money and come tell Bowl and me about the whole thing. Anyway, we took off two such cocaine dealers for a lot. The first such heist was in San Geronimo Valley of western Marin County. The "mark" was this skinny cocaine dealer who thought he was a rock star. He had a band, but they sucked. We got the info on him from some other dealer that had been burned on a big coke deal by the skinny rock star, so he put me and Bowl onto him.

We were just going to do a "drive-by" of the place to do a little recon, but when we heard the sounds of the band practicing in the basement, we had the inside info about the powder's location, so the saying of no time like the present fit. We figured that the stash was located in a top-floor bedroom. We quickly parked Bowl's Chevy, and with our pistols in hand, we made our way onto the property. All doors were locked, and making noise to gain entry would have certainly alerted attention. How many people were in the basement we did not know. Bowl noticed a second-story window wide open with a large oak tree we could use for access to the window. We acted fast, hoping not to confront anyone. We made it to the master bedroom, and, damn it if the drugs weren't right there where they were said to be, along with a very nice 357 Magnum revolver.

We made our way downstairs to exit the place, and Bowl closed the door to the basement where the noise was coming from and locked the deadbolt. I grabbed us a couple of cold beers from the fridge and walked out the front door with over twenty thousand dollar's worth of cocaine. It was a large score for me because I purchased my first Harley Davidson motorcycle with some of the proceeds. I was nineteen years old, and I was the proud owner of a 1962 Harley Panhead.

It didn't matter in the least how I got it. My stock in the motorcycle world grew, and that was fine with me. Our next sour drug deal involved working out of a carpet warehouse across from the hoods that the skinny rock star/drug dealer hired to seek revenge on me and Bowl—what a racket! Anyway, we found ourselves on the roof of this carpet warehouse. It was a two-story structure, but at the peak of the steeple-shaped roof, it was more like three or four stories high, and that's where we were trying to pry open a skylight. It was about 1 am. As far as we could tell, the skylights were not alarmed. The alarm system was visible on the first-floor doors and windows. After prying and beating the skylight for over an hour, the whole thing finally came loose—frame and all. We slowly slid the entire skylight, frame, and glass to the side of the hole it covered. The skylight glass was the kind you couldn't see through, but now we could see through the skylight-sized hole that there was at least a forty-foot drop. Right below the skylight-sized hole was a maze of flimsy-looking rafters hanging from the ceiling, and below that was more than a three-story drop. Naturally, we had no rope, so we climbed down onto the maze of creaking, flimsy rafters. If we could make it a distance of about forty yards on these rafters, we could drop down onto the roof of the office section inside the warehouse. So here we were, friggin' shitting our pants, trying to make our way across these rafters. Now, I love Bowl, and we had lived through a lot of shit together that we shouldn't have, but it never failed: when we were on a heist together, we would argue about how to do things right up to the point of almost throwing blows. Here we were, some forty feet off the ground, moving like a couple of shaky sloths, arguing about the situation we were in. We made it over the roof of the inside offices without killing each other. We made a couple of crude ropes out of our belts and a jacket, for it was still a good twenty-foot drop to the roof of the offices. We both landed on the office roof one by one with a large thud. Even with the crude rope, it was still a fifteen-foot drop. We never saw our jackets or belts again; they remained behind, hanging from the rafters for the enemy to find. There was an air conditioning unit on the roof of the inside offices. We made short work of the air conditioner and gained entry to the offices. We weren't positive about the presence of a motion alarm, so we went through the place like a friggin' meteor! We found drug scales, baggies, and all sorts of paraphernalia, but no drugs. We had already been in there too long. I looked behind a small desk in the corner, and Bowl said, "I looked their Tyke. Nothing there but a garbage bag."

Having to look for myself, I opened the garbage bag, and what did I see but two pounds of kick-ass cocaine! This was back in the days when cocaine was going for over two thousand dollars an ounce. Sixteen ounces to a pound, two pounds—you do the math! It was time to go! As I did the math, even before we left the building, I remember thinking about how I could buy a new Harley every half hour! We weren't positive about the motion alarm inside the offices, but we were sure that our exit would be loud. Surprisingly, this was the first thing all night that Bowl and I didn't argue about. So, the plan was simple: walk right out the front door like we owned the place and run like hell. We parked Bowl's Chevy about three miles away, and out the front door we went. The alarm went off immediately as we were picking up our foot speed. Now, Bowl could run like a friggin' deer. He still holds the long jump record at Novato High School, and playing the outfield my whole life, I wasn't slow, but at 2:30 in the morning, two career criminals running through the streets of downtown San Rafael with an alarm going off in the background, carrying two pounds of cocaine—it was no surprise we made good time. We made it to a safe house and mapped out our next move.

You might think that with a score of about seventy thousand dollars, we were well on our way to every day being Saturday night. You're close, but two career robbers who, overnight, become drug dealers with plenty of premium products find that word spreads far and wide with such hot news, and nothing spreads faster than bad news. With Bowl and me, good news for us usually meant bad news for someone else. Our gain equaled their loss. Either way, this kind of talk brings heat from the cowards we robbed. Inquiries were being made into who boosted the cocaine. The criminal network that was being searched by the cowards we robbed once again turned out to be our friends, so no one ratted! Yee-Ha! Saturday, Saturday, Saturday nights, alright! Chrome parts for the Harley and Bowl and I bought Monte Carlos. I rented a two-bedroom condo in Novato, bedded down a different lady every night, and, without a care in the world about the future, I partied until the money ran out. I figured, why get a job when all I had to do was "pull a job"? To me, it was absolutely ridiculous to stop partying, go home to get a good night's sleep, wake up early, and earn an honest living at an honest job. This deranged thinking of mine went on for almost half a century.

CHAPTER 5

From Tehachapi to Tracy

Back then, I had hundreds more felonies to commit and over twenty-five years in prison to serve. As embarrassing as this life of mine has been to admit, my dedication to a life of crime, I believe, was somewhat like an illness that even long stays in prison could not cure. There were countless felonies committed even inside prison. I'll get into crime behind bars later in the story. I was twenty years old in 1980 and about to be sent to state prison. The big cocaine proceeds had run dry, so I jumped back into the jewelry theft trade, but right off the bat, I messed up. I got careless on a heist in the city of Corte Madera. I was pinched by the Marin County Sheriff's Department, leaving the robbery. I had been seen going in and drove out right into a roadblock. I was booked into Marin County jail. The evidence against me was overwhelming; a bullet wound would've been less painful. I did, however, have my first encounter with Marin County District Attorney Kit Mitchell. She was a small, petite woman who carried herself with confidence. She was previously employed as a state parole officer before joining the District Attorney's office. She was well-educated in the ways of the repeat offender. Over the years, I'm sure Kit disliked me, but something about her always curled my toes. Even when she was trying to send my Irish butt to prison for the rest of my life, I'd dream about getting her on the back of my Harley. Is that weird? I don't care! She had a cute lil' butt.

Anyway, I pled guilty to the Corte Madera heist and threw myself at the mercy of the court. I was looking at either a sentence of sixteen months, two years, or three years. I got three years in California's state prison system. I was sent to a medium-security prison in the Tehachapi Mountains just east of Bakersfield, California. Life in Tehachapi prison was not as bad as most prisons, but shit happens in prison, especially in the mornings. I had been at Tehachapi prison for about six months when an unavoidable altercation erupted between me and an abnormally large black man nicknamed "Kong" in the prison weightlifting yard. It started as an argument over a bench press machine, but little time passed before we were throwing punches at each other. I like to think I held my own in the fight with Kong, but I don't remember much, and it got worse when the prison guards came running and the guard tower shot off a warning shot. We were chained up and dragged over to the hole. The hole is slang for segregated housing units, the jail inside the jail for unruly convicts. I had stuffed a marijuana doobie in my shoe earlier for an after-workout smoke. When I was getting booked into the hole for fighting with Kong, the guards found it in my shoe.

You might say, "Damn, Tyke, why didn't you get rid of the doobie?" Well, I would have had Kong not knocked me into an old episode of "Star Trek" with his anvil-sized fist. I could have made such a decision. So, as a result of my fun with Kong and possession of marijuana, I was transferred to a prison with higher security. I never saw Kong again, but I remember him. I was transferred to a prison named Duel Vocational Institution in Tracy, California. Tracy prison lived up to its nickname of "Gladiator School" because every day, someone was stabbed, jumped, or beaten. You never traveled alone in Tracy prison. Every chow call, yard call, or any movement at all, you went in numbers. Someone alone was a target. This place was a friggin' madhouse. The prison authorities didn't give a rat's ass about fistfighting; you only got into trouble if you stabbed someone. I spent a year and a half there.

I paroled in 1982 with a black eye and two hundred dollars. I was 22 years old with a 17-year-old's mind. All my parole plans consisted of were motorcycles and motorcycle chicks. After reuniting with my family while the battery on my old Harley was recharging away in my parent's garage, I put gas and oil in the old Pan Head. My parents' place was up on a steep hill. I pushed off from the driveway like I was setting off to sea. I tried to start the old Harley by compression on my parents' hill, and it complied halfway down. I was off in search of my second prison term. The two hundred dollars I got from the state for graduating gladiator school didn't even last until dark, so less than twenty-four hours out of prison, plans were being developed in my mind for the next heist. Finding legal employment was the furthest thing from my seventeen-year-old way of thinking. Anyway, I teamed up once again with Bowl, this time in pursuit of the precious metal trade. The price of gold in 1982 was over eight hundred dollars an ounce. Bowl and I sailed like a couple of pirates seeking treasure to plunder. For the next two years, I was involved in more heists than I could ever remember.

Thinking back, I can find comfort in only one thing throughout my lifetime of crime: I never physically hurt anyone. I'm not sure if that will keep me from going to hell, but I like to think so. I know I've frightened a few folks with my stupidity, and if any of those people should read this book, First, I'm sorry! Second, damn, I was scared too. Alright, back to 1982. Bowl and I hit a jewelry store I had been casing a few years earlier. The store had a moveable safe with some sort of heavy-duty dolly. We went in for a little recon of the jewelry store located in Sausalito, California. The same safe was there, and our plans for a smash-and-grab heist were set. Bowl's electronic skills didn't cover jewelry store alarm systems. The back of the jewelry store was perfect for what I had in mind. There was a heavy-duty metal door with a metal door frame and two good-sized deadbolt locks. It was a one-story building with two stairs leading up to the back door.

We stole a Pontiac Bonneville the night before the robbery, and my plan was this: We opened the engine compartment hood, and on the driver's side front inside the wheel well, we used claw hammers to expose the front left tire. We grabbed an eight-foot-long railroad tie lying by a lumber yard in San Rafael and drove to the back of the jewelry store. With a decent-sized rope, we tied the railroad tie to the front left fender of the stolen Pontiac, making sure at least four feet of the railroad tie protruded beyond the front bumper. We looped the rope around the fender, securing the wood in place and avoiding any rubbing of the tire on the rope. With the inside wheel well gone, there was plenty of clearance, and we were still able to close the hood, further securing the rope. In short, we made a medieval battering ram out of a Pontiac. We were ready.

Bowl made his way to a phone booth two blocks away and made a diversion call to get the on-duty police officers moving in a different direction. He returned four or five minutes later with a smile and a thumbs-up. He manned the heavy-duty dolly. It took two attempts, but the Pontiac/battering ram worked perfectly. Bowl was already moving inside with the dolly. We had maybe three or four minutes to get this done. I swung the Pontiac around and backed up right to the busted door until the back bumper touched the building. I jumped over the trunk, popped it open, and ran inside the jewelry store to help Bowl. He already had the safe on the dolly, but it was too heavy for him to handle alone. We almost had to give up and abandon the mission. The safe was easily four or five hundred pounds. We were burning up way too much time trying to get it to budge, but we had to give it another go.

Hooray! We managed to tilt the safe back on the dolly's wheels and started to move it. The plan from this point was to roll the safe fast enough to jump the back threshold and land it inside the Pontiac. With a two-step rise to the back door, we had plenty of room to clear the back bumper of the Pontiac. We just had to gather enough speed with the safe on the dolly. Well, we Evil-Keneviled the safe inside the Pontiac's trunk, but we ruined the rear of the car in the process. With no time to spare, we jumped into the car and slowly got going.

Most vehicles used the two main ways into Sausalito and the same two ways out, so we climbed the hill that the town of Sausalito is built upon and accessed Highway 101 from there. Halfway up the hill, we stopped, jumped out, and cut the ropes that still held the railroad tie to the front left fender. We used some of the cut rope to tie down the trunk hood since we had destroyed any chance of it working properly ever again. At this point, I remember looking back at the downtown area of Sausalito and seeing police scrambling all over. Bowl and I looked at each other over the roof of the Pontiac, exchanged a couple of grins, and jumped back in the car to drive to my buddy's machine shop to crack open another safe. We collected a little over fourteen thousand each for our efforts that night.

A few months later, Bowl got pinched for a home invasion robbery in Mill Valley. I was back to making moves on my own, and word spread, as it always did, about my one-man crime spree. Remember, nothing spreads faster than someone else's bad news! The Marin County Police Department had me dialed in as a suspect in just about every crime that occurred there. My old girlfriend Dish was away at college by this time, and I would come back to town after a week or so of visiting her at school and hear all the rumors about what I must have done. One felony after another without even being in town, but make no mistake, those rumors had a foundation.

It wasn't long before some "rat" got into a tight spot with the cops and gave them my name as the responsible person in a couple of local heists in exchange for leniency. This came to my attention one day with no warning. I was driving through San Rafael, still in 1982, and saw a San Rafael police car coming my way in the opposite direction. With my jewelry business in full swing at the time, I certainly paid attention to any sightings of the police. We passed each other, going in opposite directions, with the officer eyeing me as we passed.

What was unknown to me at the time was that this rat, who had shared my name with the cops for leniency, had also given them the locations and dates of several heists that he knew I had been a part of because he had also been involved. He failed to tell the cops that part. Anyway, after that, a warrant was issued for my arrest. I watched the curious San Rafael cop in my rearview mirror after we passed in opposite directions, just long enough to see him pull a quick U-turn and throw on his cop lights and siren. With no doubt in my mind that he was after me, I quickly made a series of turns and got out of his sight, but only for a moment.

I bailed out on foot, completely abandoning my truck and life as I knew it. I was in the town of Terra Linda and knew the area well. On foot, this San Rafael cop would need help, and he got plenty. I had no choice but to begin a series of backyard hops. Every time I came to an opening where I could see a break to an open space or hillside, another police cruiser would appear with lights and sirens, and I'd be backcrossing neighborhoods, backyard to backyard. At the time, I didn't know exactly why they were after me, but with the effort and manpower being spent on this pursuit, I was sure the reason equaled prison. It was still an hour until I would have the cover of darkness.

In that frantic hour, they had me boxed in a couple of times. I had to leap from a fence top to the roof of a house at one point to let three pursuing officers continue into the next backyard, thinking they were on my trail. I watched from the roof of the house as they grunted and groaned, trying to apprehend me. I double-backed but soon gathered another trio of officers. The Marin County Sheriff's Department had also joined in on the pursuit. The three new San Rafael officers I gathered were in much better shape than the ones I lost hiding on the roof. One San Rafael cop, in particular, was a track star. I kid you not! We both pulled away from the other two and then altogether on a nearby hillside, but the track star cop stayed with me for better than twenty minutes. I finally lost him after a few more backyards.

I never found out that officer's name, but he almost ran me down, and back then, I had never been run down in a foot race. Years later, I asked an old San Rafael police sergeant, Mike Kelly, whom I've known my whole life, if he knew this San Rafael cop. Mike Kelly just smiled at me and said, "He almost ran you down, didn't he, Tyke?" I said yes. Anyway, darkness fell and saved my freedom, but only for a while. The entire town of Terra Linda was wide awake that evening. I took refuge in a friend's garage without his knowledge. I spent the night in that garage, listening to police cars racing up and down the street all night. I slept surprisingly well. I was awakened by my friend's father starting his car to go to work. I popped up as if I had just arrived and asked for a ride. My friend's father worked over in the East Bay, and that was fine with me. Over on the other side of the bay, I was able to rent a room at a cheap motel, take a shower, wash my only set of clothes, buy a bottle of rum, and try to figure out my next move. I made a few calls and found out what the cops wanted me for, and right away, I knew who had ratted me out to them. But that made no difference now. Being an ex-convict meant I was on parole at the time, so not only would I be wanted by the police but also by the state parole authorities. Life "on the run" means two things: 1. Your butt is going to jail. 2. Until number one happens, anything goes!

CHAPTER 6

On the Run

I sat in this motel room, staring out the window, contemplating and planning with both the warmth of the rum and larceny in my heart. Shit was going to happen, and damn it, if the beginning of what turned out to be an eighteen-month run from the law didn't come to me right where I sat in that motel, staring out the window. From where I sat inside my motel room, I could see a row of phone booths next to a rather large gas station and mini-market.

In 1982, way before the cellular phone explosion, people used pay phones, and I noticed most drivers stopping to use the pay phones would leave their keys in the car's ignition, and I happened to need wheels. With my status in the world being pushed up to fugitive, anything goes. The location was perfect. I was minutes from two Bay Area bridges. In broad daylight, I pulled my favorite San Francisco Giants hat real low, held my head down, and got my target in sight as he walked quickly toward the idling 3/4-ton red Chevy pick-up. The soon-to-be ex-owner was arguing on the phone as I jumped into the driver's seat of the pick-up and made it my own. I barreled out of the parking lot, in charge of nothing but trouble. I made my way undetected across the Richmond-San Rafael Bridge right back to Marin County, only a mere forty-eight hours after my headline-grabbing chase with the sheriff's department.

I headed right for the jewel of the county, the town of Tiburon. No, screwing around; I needed a score, and it had to be a good one. I was in need of a little traveling money. I made my way back onto Belvedere Island, where I had gone plenty of times before. I cruised the private streets like a villain. I came across a three-story place showing all the signs I always looked for in a heist. I parked my stolen pick-up a couple of blocks away. I made my way back to the target. I was on the front porch, listening for any sound coming from inside. After a couple of minutes, I heard nothing. I pounded on the door and rang the bell, then listened again. Nothing. I didn't see any signs of an alarm, which was unusual for this area. My plan didn't include staying too long anyway. I put my shoulder into the front door with all my two hundred pounds behind it. I burst through the front door, with the threshold splitting south as it always did. Once I regained my balance after my explosive entrance, I quickly checked for any existing alarm system. Nothing. Nevertheless, my plan stayed the same: make quick work of this heist and get into the wind. I flew up the stairs to the master bedroom to first look for a jewelry box and all portable valuables. I bagged what looked to be a large amount inside the jewelry box, which included a couple of decent watches.

I was searching for signs of a safe, which didn't appear. I made it downstairs to the dining room area. At that time in 1982, stamped sterling silver was going for nineteen dollars an ounce on the commodities exchange market. A flatware set could easily bring three thousand dollars. I found a beautiful set in the dining room cabinets. I was on my way out when I stopped and saw a key rack hanging on a wall in the kitchen next to a door that looked to lead to a garage. I stopped once again when I found some Mercedes-Benz car keys. My eyebrows rose with thoughts of what might be through this garage door. I opened the door with a Christmas morning sort of feeling. And honey, hush! A gold-colored 350SL convertible with a little over eight thousand miles on it. Brand new and yummy! It was time to upgrade. I put the jewelry box and silver flatware set in the passenger seat, then ran upstairs to the master bedroom. If the cops weren't surrounding the place by now, they weren't coming. I packed an overnight bag I spotted earlier with some clothes that looked like they would fit and went back downstairs to the garage. I threw the bag in my new car and noticed a refrigerator in the garage. I opened the fridge and helped myself to a half-case of Henry Weinhardt's beer.

I added the beer to my haul, went around the Benz, and climbed into the driver's seat. I had to adjust the seat; the previous owner must have been short. I started the car, then fished around in the glove box for the electric garage door opener, found it, hit the open button and checked the gas gauge—full—cool. I had the garage doors open and still no sign of the law. I backed my new Benz out into the wide open. I hit the close button on the electric garage door control; you can never be too careful. I never saw the red 3/4-ton Chevy pick-up again, but I would hear about it later—big time! I was two miles from the heist, sitting at a red light, and I hit the switch for the electric convertible top. It came down smoothly into a beautiful hidden compartment. I reached into the glove compartment, took out a killer pair of Ray-Ban sunglasses, slipped them on, punched on the radio, and blasted across the Golden Gate Bridge on a bright sunny afternoon, listening to

"Sympathy for the Devil" by the Stones. What a colossal prick! I can get into more detail on this heist because it's all a matter of public record. I would spend a lot of years in prison for this crime wave, but not yet.

I was at the beginning of more than eighteen months as a fugitive and more than fifty thousand miles to put on my new Mercedes. I got into San Francisco before business hours ended. I was able to fence all the goods. It was time for a little road trip. I made my way through the city, got on the Bay Bridge, and headed north on Highway 80. I was headed to Northern California State University, where my beloved Dish attended school. Dish was a very pretty lady and a bit of a party girl. It breaks my heart when I think about it, for I knew she slept around a lot, but so did I, and loving her like I did, I didn't care. So, on and off for more than thirty-five years, I loved her. I still do today. I made it to her apartment around midnight. She lived a few blocks from campus, and it was a school night, but I showed up with all the party favors and magically turned the school night into a Saturday night. I stayed with Dish for a little over a week. On the last day of my stay with Dish, while she was attending class, I went to work. By lunchtime that day, I had the local authorities spinning their wheels all over town.

It was about 10:30 am, and I found myself on the front porch of a beautiful two-story estate inside a country club community with a golf course lining the middle of this neighborhood. I half-heartedly came to the conclusion that no one was inside with the usual process of elimination by pounding on the front door hard or making a racket with the doorbell, then listening for any movement. I heard nothing but silence. This place was alarmed, turns out, well alarmed. The alarm's key panel was just inside the front door, as I could plainly see through a side window. No question about the game plan—smash and grab job! As I've always said, these kinds of heists were always good hits. When doing this type of robbery, the more sophisticated the alarm system, the better the haul because the owners of such an estate are usually confident about leaving valuables inside. With the alarm panel's red light on, indicating the alarm was indeed active, I gained entry with all of my weight—splitting north to south—yet another front door threshold. With no time to waste, for I could hear the electric buzzing sound of the alarm, telling me to punch in the code or, in about sixty seconds, the authorities would be notified. Well, I didn't have the code for the alarm, but I did have sixty seconds. I cleared the stairs with three leaps, and yee-ha! The confident estate owners left me a crime. I drove away as slowly and smoothly as my stressed self would let me. I wasn't finished just yet, and I didn't even know it. I must have been racing to answer the alarm.

I was maybe eight miles from the heist when I passed six or seven patrol cars flying right by me in the opposite direction and drove past another beautiful place, I had been eyeballing a couple of days earlier when Dish and I were out to dinner. I made a mental note of the place because there was a brand-new, seventy-thousand-dollar Jaguar parked in the driveway. Yabba, Daba, Do! With the police busy on the other side of town, I grabbed a pillow from the bed, discarded the pillow, and on the other side of town, dared I make such a nuisance of myself? Hell yes! I slipped the pillowcase over the jewelry box. I headed back downstairs. The backyard of the place had the fourth hole fairway of the golf course running behind it. This would provide perfect cover for a daylight escape on foot. As I made it to the first floor, I heard the electric buzzing of the alarm kick into another gear with a louder buzzing noise, which told me it was time to go. I made my way through the dining room, and as I was winging open a sliding glass door for my backyard exit, I stopped as I eyeballed a killer-looking display of china plates inside a cabinet. I remembered the price of silver.

Surely, a few short seconds hunting through this cabinet for a silver flatware set couldn't hurt. Sure enough, I found one. I tucked the wooden-cased flatware set under my arm and, with the bagged jewelry box, made my way to the fourth-hole fairway on this golf course. It had to have been at least a par four or five because my escape took me all the way to the green. It was a good long distance, clinging and clanging all the way like friggin' Santa. My Mercedes was parked just off the fifth hole's tee in a small parking lot, looking all along like it belonged parked in this residential country club, except for the one minute my hoodlum self-jumped inside it with stolen goods tucked under both arms. The car would never have been suspected of aiding in a crime. I just drove straight into the driveway of the place because up close to the garage, I was completely hidden from the street with lots of trees and bushes. I once again made my way onto a front porch that didn't belong to me. I got down in my best San Francisco Niners fullback stance and gained entry through the front door.

CHAPTER 7

A Thief's Holiday Season

I collected my second jewelry box of the morning. After I drove away from the Jaguar estate with the burglar alarm buzzing away, I thought this might be a good time to skip town. I called Dish a couple of hours later when I stopped for a bite to eat in Sacramento. I was running a story by her that I had things to do back in the Bay Area and that I would come to see her again in a couple of weeks. She said okay, but before we said goodbye and hung up the phone, she mentioned how all the cops in town were flying up and down the local streets for some reason. I told her that I hate it when that happens. We sighed and said our goodbyes, but I know Dish, and she knows me, so the insecurity inside me had me calling her back that night. I mainly wanted to poke around for any more information on the police activity. When I got Dish on the phone, it was big news. She told me about all of the crazy police activity going on around town. She said the cops were in pursuit of someone or some people. They were scouring the town, busting everyone's balls, and jacking up all the local hoods. She said it was the talk of the town. She gave me a kind of fake cocaine laugh, and I knew right then she knew somehow, I was responsible for the police commotion. I let a couple of months go by before I went back to visit Dish. A couple of weeks just didn't seem long enough to let the dust settle. I just couldn't stay away, though; that babe had me.

As I hung up the phone after talking to Dish to shake the lousy feelings of being who I was, I just said to myself, as I always did when I was feeling lousy about doing such crimes, there I go again, stimulating the local economy. With the news Dish provided about these estates already reporting hundreds of thousands of dollar's worth of property missing, the real total was maybe fifty to sixty thousand dollars' tops. The estate owners make money, the police, in a way, keep their job security, the alarm company will be involved in more security, and the insurance companies will raise their premiums. In my twisted mind, I believed I was doing some good, or at least, that's how I talked myself out of those lousy feelings. It was now getting close to the holiday season of 1982. I love Christmastime in San Francisco. Wanted by more than three police departments and the state parole authorities, but that didn't stop me from feeling the warmth of the holiday season. Even in the cold San Francisco weather, the downtown Christmas season spirit is my favorite.

It had already been on the local news channel how two estates had been burglarized of hundreds of thousands of dollars' worth of jewelry. Christmas was about a week away, and I was almost broke. Being broke was a dangerous place for me. I parked the now almost-year-old Mercedes at a Mill Valley motel parking lot. I stole a small Toyota pick-up truck from a nearby shopping center that morning as I left town with the top down, smoking a doobie.

A lifelong friend of mine was getting married, and I was asked to be in the wedding party as an usher. It was a bit of a tiptoe time for my Irish butt. The wedding was being held in a church down the street from the San Rafael police department. but weddings always equaled a 101 across the Golden Gate Bridge and on into the city of San Francisco. I drove up to one of the more affluent neighborhoods named Pacific Heights. This is a very nice area. Now, back in 1982, folks still stuffed Christmas cards with cash.

I found two United States mailboxes on the corner of two streets jam-packed with mansions and beautiful estates. I went to an all-night hardware store where I purchased a hacksaw and two packages of blades. It took nearly all night to cut those friggin' cast iron mailboxes off their stands. In between darting out of the sight of passing headlights and snobs walking their poodles, I had both mailboxes in the back of my stolen Toyota pick-up around 1 am. With it still just one week before Christmas, I figured I would do all right money-wise after I beat the boxes open. I know, I know, I'm a prick. When I told my younger brother about the heist, he called me a true-life "Grinch." I said, "Ah, shut up. You got your Christmas present out of the loot." This heist will haunt me.

With every new version of the movie "The Ghost of Christmas Past," I picture myself as Scrooge. Before I leave this world, I would like to make up for this heist. I've gone to church a couple of times and went to confession with this crime included in my list, but I'm pretty sure heaven is still holding this one against me. It was Christmas time, after all. I drove back across the Golden Gate Bridge into Marin County, took the Lucas Valley exit, and made it out to the rural hills of western Marin County's dairy ranches. I pulled out on a dirt road up by Big Rock and beat them with a sledgehammer until dawn. I got just over fourteen hundred dollars for that sin. With the holidays over and 1983 just beginning, my Mercedes and I were still hot as hell. I tried to take advantage of the winter months, pulling small heists here and there. I would call the winter months the felony season because it turns dark earlier, and any serious crook does his best work in the dark. I had already put way more mileage on the Mercedes than the previous owner. My popularity was losing its appeal. The police had tried to turn up the heat in their pursuit of me, even going so far as to interview my friends' parents. Me coming around meant trouble for all. I would come back into town after being up north staying with Dish, and I would go around the few places that I still could without bringing any trouble to anyone. I would hear about all the rumors that were circulating about me. The police were holding me responsible for robbing places I didn't even know were worth robbing. I chalked it up to the fortunes of war. I was even blamed for robbing a cocaine dealer that I liked and had sold cocaine to earlier. This clown was so torn up from his own products that he told everyone it must have been Tyke who robbed him at gunpoint. Well, it turns out that it was his brother-in-law who robbed him. I could feel my time was running out. I was low on traveling money, and summer was upon me. I'd been checking from time to time on a nice-looking new housing project going up just south of the Tiburon exit on Highway 101. It sure looked ripe with all the new estates now occupied.

The residential town was named Strawberry Point. The only trouble was that there was only one way in and out. On foot, it would take all night just to get to the area I needed to get to while remaining undetected. I drove in to do a little recon from the front seat of my Mercedes. It was maybe four miles before I came within sight of any of the estates, and there wasn't a bad-looking palace anywhere to be found. All of them were friggin' million-dollar mansions. This was truly a pirate's hunting ground. I drove back out of Strawberry Point still without an approach plan. Pretty "chesty" of me doing recon work in a place where it was stolen a year earlier. Anyway, I had a heist to do, and the plan was for the Mercedes 350 SL to be not more than a couple of baseball throws away from the needed work. I went to a bar/restaurant named Zack's in the city of Sausalito. From the back porch at Zack's, I could have a couple of beers while looking across Richardson Bay and see the south side of Strawberry Point like a cat eyeballing a mouse. I was sitting at a table working on my second beer, staring across the fish aquarium, when two guys cruised by on kayaks. I said, "Damn, I can do that?" Well, as much as I liked to fancy myself a modern-day pirate, it turned out that I'm not very seaworthy, but that didn't stop me. After the day began to turn dark, I stole a kayak and one of those double paddles from a kayak rental place where the two guys I spied from Zack's head. Once I literally saw that the "coast was clear," I cast offshore with my heist backpack on and immediately rolled the kayak upside down and almost drowned in three feet of water. I didn't give up, though. It was about 8:30 pm, and it really was Saturday night. With summer in full swing, Saturday night was prime time for crime.

Soaking wet, I got the kayak turned upright, grabbed the paddle, climbed back in, and shoved off once again. I took it slow this time, and I sort of got the hang of it. I was a little tipsy from the beer, but after falling into the Bay water, I was instantly sober. Frisco Bay water is friggin' freezing. So here I was, not knowing what was waiting for me on the other side of this Bay, rowing myself to financial freedom as I saw it anyway. About halfway across, the wind started to blow and rocked me around pretty well.

CHAPTER 8

A Safe Bet Gone Wrong

About halfway across, the wind started to blow and rocked me around pretty well. I was reminded of the movie "The African Queen," with Bogie and Hepburn out on the water, getting blown around by the weather, trying to torpedo the battleship. I wasn't any Humphrey Bogart, but I was a torpedo. The wind died down a bit as I got closer to the shore of Strawberry Point. And with the water calmer I began to maneuver the kayak a little better. I skimmed along the shoreline about twenty feet out, reconning the backyard and private docks of some seriously nice-looking places. Tennis courts, huge wooden decks, and beautifully manicured landscapes as far as the eye could see. I slowed at the sight of a beautiful sailboat tied to a private dock with all the latest water sports equipment. There was a boathouse with two new jet skis and a small speed boat. I coasted the kayak to the corner of the dock and quietly reached out and grabbed the dock with my hand to steady myself. There were two people just now retreating from the pier, stepping onto the stairway that led up to the estate where a rather large party was in full swing.

The couple was laughing and tangled up in each other's arms. I watched as they disappeared into the party crowd. There was a live band blasting away with dance music and a lot of people having a good time. I looked behind me towards the estate next door. Surely a party of this size would warrant an invitation to the neighbors? So, I backed my kayak up to get a closer look at the neighbor's place. I made it to what looked like the property line in between the two estates and went ashore. The properties had plenty of trees and bushes right down to the water line, providing plenty of coverage for me and the kayak. I pulled the kayak on shore into the cover of trees. Even though this kayak was just a single seater, it was like twenty-five feet long.

I found out later that these long-built kayaks are made that long to handle better out in open water. Anyway, I made my way up the property line until I had a clear view of residences. The neighbor's estate next to the party house looked ripe and the party house was plenty busy. No lights were on over at the neighbors as I crept closer. I passed a tool shed on the inside of the neighbor's place with an extension ladder hanging off the side.

As I closed in on the neighbor's estate, I could see that it was very nice, and no movement inside as far as I could tell. I was up on the back porch, now, making my way around the place, when the kitchen lights sprang on. I dove off the back porch, falling blindly into the dark. I landed on some Juniper bushes and caught a branch right in the side. I whimpered there for a minute because it friggin' hurt big time. My side was killing me, so I took a breather by the tool shed. With the neighbor's home, this place was off the hit list. From where I now stood by the tool shed, I had a good view of the party house. On the second floor of the party house, I could see a window half open with no one inside the room and no lights on at all on the top floor. I looked to my left and saw the extension ladder hanging on the side of the tool shed. As the plan started to form in my head, the pain in my side went away. Nothing like a well-planned felony to cure what ails you. Well, for me anyway. Even though the plan was pretty simple-make my way through the window, grab what's grabbable, and get gone. It didn't quite go according to plan, but my side did not hurt me anymore. I nabbed the extension ladder and made my way to the part of the party house directly below the open window.

I anchored the ladder into a flowerbed, or I thought I anchored it? Anyway, there was a fence that ran from the middle of the estate to the property where I was separated from the party. I then extended the ladder, but it was around five feet short of the window. I was sure that I could hit by sanding on the very top of the ladder. I was just about to start climbing up the ladder when I could feel with my feet that the flowerbed was wet and spongy. I thought I was anchored well enough, and I was almost to the top of the ladder, and the friggin' ladder started to sink in the soil to the right downhill side. I quickly got that stomachache feeling of "Fuck me. I'm done for." Out of nowhere, with no thought at all, I grabbed hold of the ladder and, with all of my weight and strength, hopped like I was on a giant Pogo stick. The ladder and I went up about four or five inches, came back down, and found solid ground. It scared the shit out of me! I remember John Belushi doing the same thing in the movie. "Animal House," as he was spying on some babes in their sorority house. It turned out so well for Belushi, but that night, I made it to that window. I pulled my criminal ass inside the window to what appeared to be a spare bedroom. No signs of everyday life but smartly furnished. Gloves already on, I masked up just in case I ran into anyone. I was just gonna high-tail it back to the good shit, but I didn't need anyone to identify me in the process. The door in the spare bedroom was closed so I opened it just a crack to get a look. The upstairs hallway was clear of anyone and I could see all the way across the hallway to what was most likely the entrance to the master bedroom with double doors leading to the back of the estate.

Halfway down the hallway from where I now stood, the hallway turned into a sort of balcony that overlooked the downstairs living room. A lot of party noise was coming from that exact location. I started for the master bedroom anyway. A few feet from where the hallway became a balcony, I got down on my belly and made like a serpentine crocodile. From the angle on the floor, I couldn't be seen from down below in the living room. I made it to the double doors, and I could stand back up. If I took one big step back the way I came, I would be exposed to the crowd below. With both gloves and a ski mask on, and knowing this wasn't a costume party, I was pinned against these double doors. For just a moment, I tried to listen for any noises inside the double doors, but with the band playing, I could not tell either way. I tried the door handle. It was locked. This was both good and bad. Good-meaning possible valuables inside. Bad, meaning someone is inside the room. I pulled out my bück knife. Every con carries a knife- those are the rules. The doors were a bit flimsy, and I pushed the blade of my knife through the middle l the lock latch, like a credit card, and "Voila," it opened easily. No one was Inside. My heart rate was back up to its usual dangerous pace as I got into the meat and potatoes of most felonies. I quickly found a large jewelry box that I bagged up in my backpack. I found a safe in the walk-in closet. It was about two feet high and twenty inches wide. I tried the handle to see if it was open, but no luck.

I had hit a ranch years earlier in Napa Valley that had a nice safe inside the den. I tried the safe's handle, and it was open. Ever since then, when I find a safe, I always check the handle first. Anyway, this one was locked. I tried to move the safe, and surprisingly, it was not that heavy—maybe a hundred pounds or so. With the jewelry box already in my backpack, there was no way I could carry a hundred-pound safe. Plus, I didn't know if the U.S.S. "Get-me-outta-here" could handle the extra weight. I knew for sure it wasn't going to be long before some babe or two wandered upstairs to find a place to tinkle. I hated leaving that safe behind. With the noise of at least a partygoer in my ears, my heart was doing its best Humphrey Bogart impression, but my criminal mind was in the lead. I grabbed a worn bed sheet from the king-sized bed, laid it out by the double doors, and muscled the safe over, putting it down on top of the sheet. Friggin' safe was a bit heavier than I first thought. I circled around it and quickly fashioned a rope out of leather belts I collected from the walk-in closet. I tied the makeshift rope to the bed sheet. I took a deep breath as I reached for the bedroom door handle, ready to make my exit when—"Kablam!"—two or three girls crashed into the double doors, furiously trying to get in! I nearly jumped right through the ceiling into the damn attic! Luckily, I had relocked the doors after entering, but that didn't stop the cardiac issues I was experiencing at the moment. These ladies were dead set on getting in.

However, someone behind them said something I couldn't understand because my friggin' heart was still beating like a dirt bike engine. They gave up on the door and headed back down the stairs. I cracked open the door and saw them as they went for the stairs. I had to move quick before my friggin' heart seized up, and I was found face down, flat dead in this place. Once again, I made like a reptile across the exposed part of the hallway, all the while hanging onto the other end of my homemade rope—just enough to stay out of sight from the partygoers below. When I made it far enough to where I could rise back up on my feet, I turned back around low on one knee and started to pull my safe across the exposed part of the hallway. Surprisingly, it slid across the carpeted floor and came right to me without much of a fight. That was the only thing that went smoothly that night. I was now back in the room I deemed the spare bedroom. I was able to lock myself inside. I quickly slid the safe over to the window. I looked out the window, seeing the ladder just as I had left it. I hoisted the safe onto the windowsill and started to lower it to the ground using the rope I had made, but my rope wasn't nearly long enough. With no other choice, I had to let go, and the safe made the rest of the trip by itself. It felt like a wrecking ball, taking out two well-maintained rose bushes on impact. The safe came to rest a couple of flowerbeds away from the ladder. I got my Irish butt down there fast, grabbed the ladder, lowered the extension part with the rope pulley, and then discarded the ladder into some nearby bushes. Since the entire distance back to the boat was downhill, it didn't take long to drag the safe, but I was winded by the time I made it to the shoreline. After I caught my breath, I still wasn't sure how we were all going to fit in this one-seat kayak.

The kayak was long but also very wobbly, and the one spot to sit in only had room for one person's feet up front. The only plan I could come up with was to sit in the safe on the only seat and then sit my butt on the safe and paddle myself to the party. Sound good? Well, it did for about five whole seconds.

After I cast off from shore, with the balance of a mud wrestler, I went right into the drink, completely over my head. Somehow, the safe and backpack stayed inside the kayak. My scraped side was stinging big time from the salt water. I was already treading water, so I said, "Screw it," I'll just hang off the side of the kayak for the trip back across the bay. I had already lost the paddle in the dark water, and I was stressing that at any minute, I would hear someone yelling after discovering my heist. So off I went.

Even though it was summertime, Richardson Bay is still part of the San Francisco Bay, which is damn cold! By the time I realized this was a seriously bad idea, I was already halfway across Richardson Bay and still had a good half hour left to swim. I needed to get out of the water immediately! I was numb all over. I flipped my body over the back of the kayak and straddled it like a log. I was able to make a slightly better time this way, but I was still freezing.

Years later, I talked about this with a doctor inside prison. He was serving six years for a large fraud case. He told me that if I hadn't gotten out of the water, I would have died for sure. Considering that it took me another twenty minutes to reach shore, I believed him. I finally reached the shore on the Sausalito side of Richardson Bay and nearly passed out— I was so cold.

Hypothermia was setting in on me, and I didn't even realize it. There I was, with the kayak, the jewelry box inside my backpack, and the safe all beached on the shore. I think about thirty minutes went by before I could move. I stashed everything as best I could and pushed the kayak back out to sea. I had to walk a few miles to get back to where I parked the Mercedes. The walk made it possible to feel my hands and feet again. My clothes were dry by the time I made it back to the car. I jumped in and drove back to where I'd come ashore over an hour earlier.

I put the safe into the trunk and made my way to my old buddy's machine shop to crack open the safe. Four hours of drill press work later, I had emptied the safe of its contents: exactly six thousand dollars in cash, a .45 caliber automatic pistol, and a near-flawless marquise-cut diamond ring. I pulled a little better than eleven thousand from the contents of the jewelry box. So, hell, yes! It was party time! Like I said before, it was summer, so Dish was home from school. Dish and I loaded up the Mercedes with a couple of overnight bags, and with the top down, we blew out of town and headed for Palm Springs.

CHAPTER 9

From Palm Springs to San Quentin

We stopped at a 7-Eleven so Dish could buy some cigarettes, and I waited in the car. I noticed a newspaper stand in front of the 7-Eleven featuring the Marin County paper named The Independent Journal. Curious about what the paper said about my activities the night before, I got out of the car, fished out a couple of quarters, and bought the day's edition. On the second page of the front section was a half-page article about my work. The reporter's account was fantastic. The article read like a screenplay for an episode of Michael Mann's Miami Vice. The headline read: "Cat Burglar Baffles Authorities and Sophisticated Alarm System! Burglar Escapes with Safe and Five Thousand in Jewels!" The alarm system wasn't even activated during the party!

See, just like I always say, there I go again stimulating the local economy. I didn't care what they said about me; I was now blasting down the freeway, top-down in my stolen

Mercedes, my pockets full of cash on a gorgeous summer afternoon, with the love of my life sitting right beside me, heading to Palm Springs.

I was a friggin' modern-day pirate! Arg!! Dish and I stayed in a beautiful suite at a Palm Springs resort for twelve days and had a wonderful time. We returned to Marin County in mid-August, and Dish had to start making plans to return to school. She knew I was still wanted by the law, so there was no talk of a future together. I just told her that I would come for a visit when I could. I continued to spend money freely, so it wasn't long before I was back to no good. Both Bowl and Foud were away on prison terms. I was drinking in a bar in Cotati, California, where I was making a few calls to gain more information on a heist I knew about. The information I already had was a lead on a dope dealer who stashed his cash in a safe house. I was busy drinking rum and cokes while waiting for a return phone call to be given the address of the place.

The call came in. I copied down the address, finished my rum and coke, and strolled out to my Mercedes for the very last time. I didn't get more than a couple of miles when I was pulled over by a Cotati City squad car, for what I found out later was four miles over the speed limit. Fucking square-headed cop! I pulled over into a long dirt driveway leading to a small ranch. I raced up the driveway, creating dense dust clouds. I locked up the brakes and abandoned my Mercedes. I bolted across a couple of small pastures, but I was still two hours away from the cover of darkness. The odds were against me, and I didn't know the area that well. I thought I was doing well a couple of times, but Cotati's finest kept showing up every time I thought I was in the clear. Plus, Sonoma County sheriffs were now involved in the chase as well.

It wasn't long after I made a couple of directional mistakes before a few cops on foot herded me up against Highway 101 with the help of a couple of squad cars. I was about to cross the highway when one cop with a bead on me with his shotgun yelled out, "Don't do it, boy, unless you want a big hole in you." Well, I was out of breath and didn't want a big hole in me. Plus, the cops on foot all had their service revolvers aimed at me. Party over!

I called Sonoma County Jail home for the next seven months. Marin County authorities were knocking on the door for months, trying to accuse me of everything they could think of and then some. I hired a lawyer because they weren't going to believe a word I had to say anyway. They placed a felony "hold" on me, preventing me from posting bail, but with a no-bail hold from the state parole authorities, I wasn't making any bail anyway, so Marin County would just have to wait their turn.

I was appointed a public defender in Sonoma County Superior Court, and all this "mouthpiece" wanted to talk about was how much trouble I was in. He told me that he was being constantly approached by Marin County authorities to get us into an interview room, and I'm sure he got an earful from them. The only crime I faced in Sonoma County was the theft of the Mercedes, which carried a sentence of sixteen months to three years. My sentence was three years, the maximum.

I was sent to Vacaville State Prison to go through the reception process. This is where the prison authorities evaluate each convict to place them properly within the prison system while they serve their sentence.

The evaluation usually takes three months. I was sent back to Tracy Prison, known as "Gladiator School," once again. I still had a six-count felony hold on me from Marin County. I wasn't at Tracy Prison for more than a couple of months when I was summoned to the warden's office. I was informed that I was being transferred to San Quentin Prison in the morning. It was just before the holidays in 1984, and I was being transferred to the most notorious place on the planet. It was December 14, 1983, the day I drove through the front gates of San Quentin Prison. I'll forget a lot of things in my life, but that date will stay with me as long as I live. At that time, San Quentin Prison was at level four security—the highest level of security the California prison system had to offer. That meant California's most dangerous criminals were housed inside its barf-yellow colored walls.

I stepped off the transport bus, legs and arms chained up at what was known as the R&R (Release and Receiving) building. Release and Receiving was located in the lower yard of the prison, and that's where I began my journey with about a dozen other new recruits. The first thing I noticed was a very well-maintained baseball field. For the first time since learning I was going to San Quentin, I smiled and thought, "How bad could this place be if they like baseball?" What I didn't know at that moment was that players had been stabbed at San Quentin for making errors in baseball games. Tough league.

My years inside San Quentin prison were a learning experience I still draw from to this day, mainly during survival situations. I was housed in a cell on the third tier in West Block on the bay side, which meant out of the front of my cell, through the bars that caged me, over the gun rail that the guard used to oversee me, and out the window behind the gun rail was a great view of Mount Tamalpais. As a child, I would attend picnics there with family and friends, but as a young adult, I would rob and pillage on that beautiful mountain. "So close and yet so far" could have been my motto. The cells inside San Quentin were the smallest I'd ever seen. You could put your shoulder against one wall and reach out with your other arm to touch the opposite wall. You had to walk sideways to get from one end of the cell to the other. Years later, when I heard they were double-bunking the cells, I said, "Damn, time to go," but that didn't happen.

Anyway, here I was on my first of many days in San Quentin prison. This place truly provided everything a modern-day pirate like me required for incarceration. The cell blocks reminded me of long-ago dungeons where pirates were locked away forever after capture. Don't get me wrong, for this twenty-four-year-old Irish man, I was in a mild to serious state of shock about where I now called home.

For me, growing up just a few miles from the front door of San Quentin, it was somewhat surreal to now be living there. All the war stories I'd heard from local folks who had survived San Quentin and returned to talk about it came flooding back. Well, here I am.

At the time of my arrival, I suspected that the Marin County authorities had something to do with my transfer to San Quentin. I was serving only a three-year sentence for stealing a Mercedes Benz, and my points and security level did not require the maximum security of San Quentin. In the California prison system, points are assigned based on various factors, including criminal records, length of sentence, age, and even family relationships. The point score determines the required security level within the prison system.

Points usually come into play when a convict is trying to transfer to a prison closer to home to receive visits from family and friends. The prison administration would typically say, "No, your points don't match for such a transfer." However, if the administration wanted to move you despite your points not matching up, they would simply override the system and proceed as they pleased—much like what was happening with me at that time.

I had written a letter to my folks informing them of my arrival at San Quentin. My mom and dad's love and support were unconditional.

I've known nothing stronger my whole life. Although they were aware of my illegal activities, they still remained hopeful for their middle son's future. My brothers and my only sister were busy with their own lives. Two of my brothers had even begun careers in law enforcement, following in my father's footsteps. My sister was a surgical nurse, and all my brothers still played baseball, with one even becoming the baseball coach at our old high school. I could feel that all of my family were collectively worried about my arrival at San Quentin prison. After all, they had also grown up right outside the harsh yellow-colored walls.

CHAPTER 10

The Courtroom Chess Game

I had hit a new low — perhaps the lowest. It turns out my suspicions were correct about Marin County authorities having influence over my transfer to San Quentin. I was just two weeks into my stay when I was awoken by two large, intimidating guards standing outside my cell at four a.m., telling me, "Get dressed, convict. You're going to court." Sure enough, I was packed up, transported the eight miles, and delivered to the Marin County courthouse.

This was the first of many such rides from Quentin to the Marin County Civic Center. This first court appearance was just an arraignment hearing — informing me of the charges against me and a referral to the public defender's office for appointment of counsel. The charges included five counts of burglary, two counts of theft, and a promise of more charges to come at a later date. The promise of more charges was a nice touch. There was no doubt in my mind that my favorite District Attorney, Kit Mitchell, was responsible for that. Kit was not in court that first day, but I'm sure the young lady representing the District Attorney's office was well-schooled by Kit and would not appear in court until I was bound over to Superior Court. I'm positive she was aware that I was in the building — something that seemed to bother her.

Even though, at that moment, I was serving a three-year sentence for the theft of the Mercedes out of Sonoma County, Marin County authorities were still charging me with the same crime. The second auto theft charge was for the Chevy pickup I left behind at the Mercedes heist — which made me look like a bit of a criminal/psycho. Charges were to be filed against me soon.

Those mystery charges that were supposed to be filed later turned out to be nothing but a smokescreen. The judge sided with Kit and the DA's office, and I was hauled back to Quentin. Kit looked good in court that day, wearing a tight dress and high heels — something about that chick. Anyway, I know part of her motivation had to do with my old crime partner, Bowl. Bowl had caused a bit of trouble in Marin County Jail, and Kit knew full well that Bowl and I were partners. Bowl had been released from prison a few months earlier but was caught for some sort of robbery. While he was being held in Marin County Jail, he cut a hole in the roof, escaped, and was still at large. Plus, everyone had heard rumors about the possibility of smuggling marijuana into Marin County Jail. So, San Quentin it was for me.

Okay, sorry. At my next court hearing, I was supposed to enter a plea. The Public Defender standing next to me in court that day was a soldier. He wasn't going to be my appointed counsel — he was just there representing the Public Defender's office, but he stirred things up. He cited the problems with me being housed at San Quentin and how inconvenient it would be to represent me due to the lack of availability to meet and discuss our court strategies.

As much as I enjoyed seeing Kit Mitchell at the second court hearing, it was clear once again that she did not share the same feelings for me as I had for her. She became increasingly agitated with the argument the Public Defender was making about my inconvenient housing situation at San Quentin.

Ol' Kit started her argument by emphasizing what an escape risk I was and that they had a team of officers searching for me for nearly two years, along with the significant man-hours spent hunting me down. She then added that more serious charges were soon to be filed against me.

Those so-called additional charges turned out to be nothing more than a smokescreen, but the judge sided with Kit and the DA's office, and I was hauled back to San Quentin. Ol' Kit looked sharp in court that day — tight dress, high heels, the whole deal. There was just something about her.

Part of her motivation, I'm sure, had to do with my old crime partner, Bowl. He'd stirred up some trouble in Marin County Jail, and Kit knew full well that he and I ran together. Bowl had been out of prison for only a few months before getting picked up again for some kind of robbery. While locked up in Marin, he cut a hole in the roof and escaped — still at large. On top of that, there were plenty of whispers about marijuana being smuggled into the jail. So yeah, back to San Quentin I went.

CHAPTER 11

Playing Ball and Dodging Bullets

Life inside San Quentin was like living in a minefield. You never knew when or where things could blow up. I sort of settled into a routine. I got a job in the main kitchen, met up with a few former prison graduates, and got a tryout for the San Quentin Pirates.

The Pirates was the name of the prison's baseball team. There were a few other baseball teams inside the prison, but they were only formed so the Pirates could have practice games against them and stay in shape for the real games. Local semi-pro teams from all over the Bay Area would come inside the prison to play against us. The guards even had a team we would play from time to time, but they stunk. It was big fun to beat up on the guards' team.

Anyway, I beat out the starting center fielder for the Pirates at my tryout. That night, I had my first fistfight in San Quentin. I was relieved it was just a fistfight, although it was a knock-down, drag-out fight. I kept expecting the disgruntled ex-center fielder to pull out a knife, but he never did. Good thing because, at the time, I didn't have anything sharpened. We were lucky the guard on the gun rail didn't see the fight. In San Quentin, the guards shoot bullets into fights to break them up. He was kept busy at the other end of the cell block by the showers—probably a friggin' incompetent cop. Anyway, I lost my fistfight in San Quentin with as much honor as I could. I was still young, so I healed pretty fast, and I even collected a couple of compliments for holding my own.

The Pirates' ex-center fielder, because I took his position, was a tough Aryan Brotherhood gang member who I later found out was in prison for a double murder. I told you it was a tough league. As the season went on, this murderer and I became good friends. He was a big baseball fan.

My ability in the outfield and at the plate with a baseball bat caught the attention of a Hell's Angel motorcycle club member named R-Rick. He was a large guy and a baseball enthusiast with a special love for the San Francisco Giants.

I knew a few Angels from the Bay Area due to my lifelong interest in motorcycles, which furthered my friendship with R-Rick. R-Rick got me a job in the prison welding shop. Even though I had never welded before, I didn't care. I was just happy to be out of the kitchen. Plus, the guys in the welding shop had made a homemade pressure cooker that doubled as a still, which meant homemade booze— Pruno.

In the welding shop at that time, there were two Hell's Angels, one murderer, a couple of serious armed robbers, and three mob guys in for kidnapping. All three mobsters were from New York, and it wasn't more than a couple of weeks before I had them all knowing the words to "Oh Danny Boy," thanks to the motivation provided by prison Pruno!

These were the days in prison when no punks walked the main lines. Rapists were stabbed, and if they survived, they went into protective custody. Child molesters were dealt with more harshly; sometimes, the guards would only find pieces of them. Homosexuals were also sent to protective custody, and if you messed around with a homosexual, you were considered weak and would be sent to protective custody as well.

So let me ruin all your nightmares of convict rapes and other homosexual scenarios you've seen courtesy of Hollywood-made prison movies. If you have sex with a homosexual, it's because you are a homosexual. It doesn't matter if you're pitching or catching your fag ass is in the game and, inside prison, you're considered weak and exiled from the convict lifestyle and run off to protective custody with the rest of the homos.

I was still going to court in Marin County. My case had been bumped up to Superior Court. I was seeing Kit on every visit to court now. The authorities had me cold on the Mercedes Benz estate robbery and also the stolen pick-up truck I left behind. Leaving that stolen pick-up truck behind like I did still eats at me today and kinda puts me in the criminally insane category, plus they had me on two more robberies.

Somehow, the cops claimed they lifted my fingerprints from the scene. That's pretty impressive detective work, considering I wore gloves for every robbery I've ever done. My court-appointed lawyer was trying to negotiate a deal with the District Attorney's office. Usually, pre-trial deals are common, but in my case, the DA's office wanted to throw the book at me. They fought hard, but damn, Ol' Kit had a nice butt! The deal my attorney and I were trying to negotiate was to plead guilty to the heists they had evidence on and, in exchange, drop the other charges. Kit Mitchell wasn't budging.

CHAPTER 12

A Gamble with Time

Back at Quentin, R-Rick and I talked about my situation. R-Rick, being familiar with the same kind of fight I was in, advised that a plea deal for the charges they had evidence on was indeed my best bet. Going to trial would almost certainly result in receiving the maximum sentence. My attorney, Kit, and her boss, Joshua Thomas, seemed determined to make things as difficult as possible. My lawyer and I kept pushing for the deal right up until the morning we were scheduled to start picking a jury for the trial. We all gathered in the courtroom and made one last effort to reach a deal before the trial began. Negotiations went on for hours, and more than once, I was tempted to lean across the table that separated me, my attorney, Kit, and her boss and say, "Look, Kit, how am I ever going to get your fine self on the back of my Harley if you send me away forever?" but I kept my mouth shut. Anyone who knows me will say that's true. I ended up pleading guilty to three heists and received an additional eight years in prison.

Note: Kit wouldn't budge on credit for time served, and I won on appeal-McCarthy vs. California (penal book 1987). I did, however, have a bit of luck during all those hours in court that day if you can believe that?

The court had gone on so long that day that the judge ordered I be housed overnight in the maximum-security section of the Marin County Jail due to transportation problems or possibly lazy cops. Now, you might be thinking, "Lucky? How so?" Having been a guest at Marin County Jail plenty of times before, I had a foolproof way of getting some extras smuggled in, and I loved to smoke pot. I never really thought of smoking marijuana as breaking the law; it's much less harmful than drinking alcohol. When you deal in pot, you're dealing with people who eat and sleep. The only things in danger when you're under the influence of pot are cookies and candies. Marijuana should be legal, especially with all the good it does medically.

Anyway, back to maximum security at the Marin County Jail. Once I was confined in the maximum-security area, I asked a couple of guys who were already there if certain procedures were still in place at the jail. Once I found out all I needed to know, I had the telephone handed down to me and made a couple of calls to some local crooks. A little over six hours later, I was in possession of four balloon-wrapped packages containing a bit more than half an ounce of some killer marijuana. I can't get into too many details since I don't want to ruin the procedure for any other fellow maximum-security pot enthusiasts. Anyway, the next morning, I gathered up my eight more years and my half-ounce of pot and headed back to San Quentin. Now, inside the prison world, if you are in possession of illegal drugs, you achieve a bit of celebrity status. This can be attributed to a nationwide problem of being "institutionalized." A certain amount of celebrity status and glory for misguided crooks like me can be intoxicating for all the wrong reasons. It can backfire on you big time, and you could end up getting killed because of it. But R-Rick and I, along with a few of the fellas, had more than a few good days smoking weed and talking about bikes and babes. I told him about a motorcycle buddy I used to party with, and on occasion, we sold each other pot. I told R-Rick his name was Lock from San Francisco. At the time, Lock was on death row at San Quentin. The sixth tier in North Block is where the death row inmates were housed. Their yard was on the roof of North Block. The only time we saw a death row convict was when they might be heading to the visiting room or being escorted to the prison infirmary.

R-Rick knew Lock well; as it turns out, Lock was a member of R-Rick's crew in the Hell's Angels Motorcycle Club. To me, and from as far back as I could remember, the Hell's Angels were second to none in the motorcycle world. Hell's Angels lived life with big bites. Who wouldn't want to be a part of that world? Even square heads fantasized about racing down the freeway on a bad-ass V-Twin motorcycle wearing the famous death head patch. If they said no to such fantasies, they were either lying or too much of a coward to admit it out loud.

R-Rick told me that Lock had a pretty strong appeal going on in court. He said his club was busy organizing benefits and bike runs to raise money for Lock's new lawyer and the possibility of a new sentencing hearing. I told R-Rick about how I still owed Lock sixty dollars from an old pot deal and that he was sent to death row before I could square up with him. Something about owing sixty bucks to a Hell's Angel on death row just never sat well with me. R-Rick said to make sure to send it to him in prison as soon as I get out. I said okay.

It turns out I was able to square up with my homeboy Lock even before I got out, but I'll get to that a little later. Right now, baseball season inside San Quentin prison is about to begin, and for the second season in a row, I was the starting centerfielder for the Pirates. There wasn't much more important or serious inside prison than sports and betting. Some local semi-pro teams made annual visits to play against us. Teams like the Novato Knickerbockers, Mr. B's, and a few others. Being from the local area, it was an extra good time since I usually knew a few of the players on the visiting teams from high school or different leagues. Most local baseball players would have also played ball at one time or another with one of my brothers.

For the most part, the San Quentin Pirates baseball team stunk. Way too much arguing went on with players who thought they were good ball players but really weren't. Most of the semi-pro teams that came inside the prison to play against us were lifelong, seasoned ball players, while the Pirates were just lifers. There were a few decent ball players on the Pirates, just enough to make it a game. I didn't give a shit. I was happy to be back in the outfield, pretending I was a free man playing ball. Plus, getting to see a few guys I played high school ball with was pretty cool.

I played two more seasons with the Pirates. During that time, I attended a Willie Nelson concert on the lower yard, watched Arnold Schwarzenegger and Franco Columbo put on a weightlifting exhibition, was involved in two major riots, and lost more fistfights than I care to remember. But the day I teamed up with an Aryan Brotherhood gang member named Vince was the closest I came to losing my life at San Quentin. Vince worked with me in the welding shop. He was a full-blooded German and an absolute psycho. He had gotten into an argument with a group of black convicts who were members of a black prison gang called "The Black Gorilla Family."

The argument was over something the Black Gorilla Family wanted Vince to weld, but for some reason, Vince refused to do the welding. The argument escalated into disrespectful comments aimed at Vince. Vince and I were walking back to West Block together after work, and Vince was in a "no way of talking him out of it, hell-bent on revenge" state of mind. By the time we made it back to West Block, a friggin' elephant tranquilizer wouldn't have calmed Vince down. And just my luck, all of Vince's Aryan Brotherhood brothers were already locked in their cells. My ass, combined with a lifetime of "Murphy's Law" luck, was the only one available to back up Vince.

As we saw the Black Gorilla Family members make their way from their cells to their shower gear and start heading towards the showers, we were winding our way to the third tier, right in front of another Aryan Brother's cell, named Blue. Vince had his two arms through the front bars of Blue's cell while Blue was frantically duct-taping a knife to each one of Vince's hands.

I thought to myself, with absolutely no sarcasm, "Fuck me," while Blue was strapping medieval-looking knives to Vince's hands. The whole time, Vince was glaring at me, explaining the plan for our revenge—our revenge? Crap, I couldn't even be mad. Vince said we'd wait a couple of minutes until they made it down to the shower because the guard on the gun rail above the showers only had a shotgun, whereas the other guards carried Mini-14s, .30 caliber rifles, and, as Vince explained it, we could stand a shotgun blast better than a .30 caliber bullet.

Once again, without any sarcasm, the words "Fuck me" entered my thoughts. Blue handed me a knife and thanked me for backing up his Aryan Brother. I had no choice at this point.

In prison politics, if a convict of good standing and of the same race as you ask for your backup and you refuse, your own race will turn against you. That creates a very unsafe environment. No place enforced these politics more strongly than San Quentin.

So here I am, with a knife in my waistband, following a psycho to go handle people I wasn't mad at, under shotgun coverage because we could withstand a blast from a shotgun? Christ! I now knew what it felt like to be a drafted infantry soldier sent into battle with a low probability of survival.

As I was following this out-of-control Nazi, I felt that old, familiar sense of shock that creeps in every time I get involved in something completely out of control. I'm positive, to this day, that God reached down and guided me through the madness that happened next. We made it to the back of the cell block by the showers undetected. Vince had on a long-sleeve jacket covering the knives taped to his hands. The Black Gorilla gang members were just around the corner of the cell block, maybe twenty feet from where we stood, getting ready to take showers. I could hear their voices. Vince looked back at me with a smile. He said something in German that I didn't understand, and before I could say, "Fucking wait," he was around the corner and headed straight for the group of four Black Gorilla Family members. Determined to follow him, I was right behind him. What happened next probably saved my life. Vince ran right past the first Black Gorilla gang member and straight into the middle of the other four. I swore I heard Vince growling during the whole charge. I didn't blame Vince for running past the first Black Gorilla gang member. He was the size of my old friend "Kong," who I had a run-in with back in the Tehachapi prison days. I made my way straight for him.

CHAPTER 13

Balm! Welcome to the Big Leagues

I was maybe two steps from Kong's twin when "Blam!" I heard a gunshot right above us. A gun going off inside a San Quentin cell block is ten times as loud—like the sound of a friggin' cannon! With my attention diverted, trying to spot bullet holes, Kong's twin hit me with a fist the size of a basketball, sending me nearly all the way back to the corner we had just jumped from. "Blam!" Another shotgun blast followed, and then I heard screaming from everywhere. The few convicts who were still on the tiers gathered to check on their buddies. Then, a swarm of guards appeared from everywhere, yelling and screaming for everyone to get down!

A white guy I was friends with named Butch was close by when everything went crazy, and saw that I was a bit dizzy. Amid the commotion, he helped me walk up to Blue's cell, where I returned the knife that was still in my waistband. I managed to get back to my cell after the smoke cleared down by the shower. The next day, the results of the incident were known: the whole prison remained on lockdown.

Vince was in the prison infirmary with shotgun wounds in both legs and a handful of new charges. Two Black Gorilla Family members were also in the prison infirmary with stab wounds. The other two, plus Kong's twin, were carted off to the hole. Vince sent word thanking me for the backup. R-Rick and the Aryan Brotherhood brought me food so I could stay in my cell until the swelling went down on the side of my head, where Kong's twin hit me. In prison, if the guards see a convict with an injury, the convict gets thrown in the hole. So, when I emerged from my cell a week later, I was considered by all as someone who could be counted on. I didn't act chesty with this status. The truth, as I knew it, was that I was a scared twenty-four-year-old who, by the grace of God, got rocked by Kong's twin but stayed out of harm's way. This was more living proof that God's miracles occur in very mysterious ways.

R-Rick was pissed off at me and the Aryan Brotherhood over the whole shower incident. I thought it was because we were pals, but R-Rick always let on about the Pirates' baseball games. I missed a couple of games because of the shower incident, and as a result, we lost a couple of games. R-Rick said that was why he was pissed. I said, "Bullshit, you ol' softy."

"You were worried about me." He tried to swing at me, but I got away. A few more months went by with no trouble. The "half-time" law that came into effect in 1983 finally made its way into the prison system. Before 1983, a convict had to complete two-thirds of his sentence to be eligible for parole. The 1983 half-time law was just what it sounds like a convict was now only required to serve half of his sentence before being considered for parole. The law reduced my sentence by one year, and, in turn, my prison point score dropped. I was transferred back to Tracy Prison and sent to Gladiator School for the third time. Tracy Prison was a wild place, but I had been there before and knew what to expect. I also knew a lot of the convicts there and was a veteran of San Quentin. They didn't have a baseball team at Tracy Prison. A couple of years back, there was a big riot in the yard, and some convicts got hold of the baseball bats and used them in the middle of the riot. No more baseball at Tracy Prison. I got a job in the recreation department to allow myself plenty of access to the prison weight pile.

Lifting weights was a great stress relief and a good way to stay healthy. My job in the recreation department was perfect and came with many perks. I handed out sports equipment to the main yard through a window attached to the gymnasium. Convicts would often use me and my window to smuggle goods off the main yard and back into the cell blocks, thus avoiding the metal detectors and the gauntlet of prison guards conducting random searches. For such services, I would always get a cut. I even brewed Pruno, hidden inside the gym, and distributed it to the customers in the yard through my window like a bartender. On hot summer days, I would get ice smuggled down from the kitchen and serve wine coolers. Some of the cons started calling my window "Tyke's Pub." Anyway, things were as okay as they could be behind prison walls.

Then, the yard got word that Lock had won his appeal. He had won his resentencing hearing and had his death sentence recalled. He was resentenced to two seven-year-to-life terms, which meant he would be sent to the main population inside the California prison system to serve his new prison term. The word on the yard was that Lock was on his way to Tracy Prison. There were already two Hell's Angels club members in Tracy Prison at the time—Booger from Berdoo and Mickey from Dago. If anyone knew the truth about Lock, it was these two. I was good friends with both of them and went to see them as soon as I heard about Lock. They confirmed it. Lock had won his life back and was on his way to Tracy Prison. The place was buzzing with talk about Lock. Convicts who knew him personally were talking about getting photos with him in the prison yard, and most others had war stories about him. Being a San Francisco Hell's Angel and coming off death row, his status as top "Peckerwood" was already sealed before he even arrived. The name "Peckerwood" in prison lingo means a solid white man.

I was in my cell that night when my cellmate, J.B., said to me, "Tyke, you knew Lock on the street, didn't you?" I said, "Yes." J.B. replied, "Damn, bro, it would be cool to meet him when he gets here. Introduce us, okay?" I responded, "Fuck, man, I owe him sixty bucks. I hope he doesn't remember me!"

It was the spring of 1986 when Lock arrived at Tracy prison. He was welcomed in the yard like a celebrity. He was the Hell's Angel who beat the hangman. It was damn good news when Lock won his life back. I knew personally that Lock was a damn good person, and that day, I was hoping he hadn't changed. As I've mentioned before, the part about owing Lock sixty dollars and not being able to square up with him before he was sent to death row never sat well with me. Now, here he was in Tracy's main prison yard, saying hello to all the homeboys. I was standing in the yard, at a respectful distance, watching with J.B., when J.B. got my attention and said, "Tyke, he's looking right over here." Sure enough, Lock was focused in our direction. Once again, the words "Fuck me" flashed through my mind. He started towards us, J.B. stepped a few feet away from me, and coming in my direction was this 6'4", 280 lbs. Hell's Angel, fresh off death row, who I owed sixty dollars from an old pot deal. I was a bit concerned. He got closer, and I didn't know if I was going to get crushed or hugged. But just a couple of feet away from me, he broke out into a big grin, like he knew damn well I was sweating this out, and said, "Tyke, you old Irish drunk," and gave me a big hug.

He said his motorcycle club brother in San Quentin, R-Rick, had sent him word that I was at Tracy and to look out for me when he got there. I never saw my friend R-Rick again. The poor guy died before he could make parole. Lock asked me how much time I had left on my sentence. I told him just under three more years. He said good; we'd get a cell together. The other two Hell's Angels brothers of Lock were already celled up together. The next morning, I got an approved cell change to C Block, less than twenty-four hours after Lock hit the yard. I said goodbye to J.B. and moved in with Lock.

To this day, Lock will tell you it was the hardest three years of his sentence, but he'd be bullshitting because we had a lot of laughs. Damn, he had just finished doing five years on death row—what could be harder than that? Right, Lock? I'm going to send him a copy of this book. He's still incarcerated. It's been thirty-two years now. I would love to share the stories and good times Lock, and I had, but Lock's life is not mine to share. What I've shared so far about Lock is a matter of public record. The rest is a lot of fun to hear about, I shit you not!

Maybe I'll ask him and get permission to write a sequel to this book or add an extra chapter called "The Lock Years"? Well, anyway, I'd still have to ask. I can tell you this, though all the years I did with Lock, he never used drugs or drank Pruno. He was a pretty serious dude. I remember saying to him one time, "Come on, Lock, party a little—you're like hanging out with a cactus." It didn't go over too well.

CHAPTER 14

Old Tricks, New Problems

My younger brother John met Lock in the prison visiting room. John was attending Sacramento State University at the time, which was just a short drive up Highway 5. He was studying criminology to help jump-start his career in law enforcement, and what better research than a field trip to Tracy prison? Lock was in the visiting room, spending time with his mother, who had come to see him. John and I were sitting right next to Lock and his mother and we all enjoyed each other's company. It was a great visit. I love my little brother John and am very proud of the man he's become and what he's done with his life, just as I am of my entire family.

After the visit, my little brother walked Lock's mother out to her car like a gentleman, and it made me feel good. Time went by fairly smoothly for me during my last three years in Tracy prison. Living with Lock, I made the best of my situation behind prison walls. In the fall of 1987, I was paroled from Tracy prison at the same age I had been when I was first incarcerated—seventeen years old! That was my mental state, anyway.

Parole, to me, was like a magical fountain of youth. After being caged up for so long, when the doors of freedom swung open, I was off and running with the heart of a teenager—and, unfortunately, the mind of one as well.

All the best-laid parole plans of getting a job and keeping the drinking down to a minimum went right down the shitter as soon as the party started. It would take a repeat of prison to stop it. My brother Jim had kept my Monte Carlo for me, and my best bro Bob had stored my Harley, which meant I had wheels from day one of freedom. As soon as the Department of Corrections two hundred dollar gate money ran out, I was all recon and research on a few jewelry store heists that I had stored in the back of my mind.

I rented a dive apartment in a suburb of San Rafael, California, called Brett Harte, and it was Saturday night all over again. I teamed up with a career criminal named Dwayne, and we made plans for a heist I knew about across the Bay in Contra Costa County. Right after I was paroled from

Tracy prison, I drove over to Contra Costa County, to the town of Lafayette, just east of the Caldecott Tunnel, to see if the jewelry store, I had in mind was still in the same rob-able condition it was a few years earlier. I did a little recon, and sure enough, there was a safe that looked removable. So here I am telling Dwayne the way to go. I robbed the Sausalito jewelry store the same exact way we would rob the Lafayette store—steal a large car of any make, strap a railroad tie to the front of the car as I did previously, and ram the back door of the jewelry store to smithereens. The Lafayette store was perfect and had the same layout as the Sausalito job.

Two stairs led up to the back door, giving us plenty of margin for error as we Evil Knievel-ed the safe onto the dolly and out the back door, loading it into whatever car we boosted for the heist. All we needed was a good diversion to send the on-duty police to the other side of town while we helped ourselves to the safe. Since it was "felony season" (wintertime), we could plan the heist most any night. But we were in a holding pattern because I hadn't figured out a diversion reliable enough to ensure the patrol units would be diverted from the heist area.

I had another problem, and it was Dwayne. Although he was a good person, he was a heroin addict. Even though he was a career criminal, he had never attempted any large robberies. He would only involve himself in small-time crime, just enough to support his habit. Heroin addicts are bad for any business, but I liked Dwayne, and I always did. Dwayne was a friggin' horse of a man, blessed with an NFL lineman's physique. His younger brother even played for the San Francisco Forty-Niners. Had Dwayne's thirst for dope not taken hold of him at an early age, who knows where he could have gone? Many have said the same about me and baseball, but this sure ain't a success story.

Well, I was glad to have Dwayne along with me on this heist because I needed some seriously strong help in the estimated three to four minutes, I figured we had to successfully rob this jewelry store. The diversion I finally came up with occurred to me when we were in the town of Walnut Creek while we were getting something to eat.

While sitting inside a taco joint, I noticed a line of pool slides lined up next to a small cyclone fence at a place called Herb's Pool Service. Right next door to Herb's Pool Service was a large bank. I had a plan for a diversion. This old bowling ball I'd kept in the trunk of my Monte Carlo for years would finally be put to some good use—or some bad, depending on your perspective. I'd found the bowling ball years ago, thinking it would be cool to roll it down some steep hill, but now I had a much better use for it.

That night, we stole a Chevy Caprice and pounded out the inner wheel well, just like Bowl and I had done earlier to the stolen Pontiac in the Sausalito heist. We loaded up a twelve-foot-long railroad tie from the same lumber yard where Bowl and I had gotten the first one. I grabbed the bowling ball from the trunk of the Monte Carlo, tossed it into the stolen Chevy Caprice, and off we went across the Richmond Bridge and through the Caldecott Tunnel. We drove right past Lafayette into Walnut Creek to set up the diversion.

We went to the cyclone fence where Herb's Pool Service stored their pool slides. Dwayne and I grabbed a twelve-foot-high slide and pulled it over the fence. The slides were made of fiberglass, so they weren't too heavy. We lugged the slide behind the bank and positioned it right at a large plate glass window of the bank. We rigged up the bowling ball at the very top of the slide with a thin string and taped a Camel non-filter cigarette to the string. We made sure the slide was aimed just right, lit the cigarette, jumped back into the stolen Chevy Caprice, and headed back to our jewelry store in Lafayette. And that's where we now sat.

We gave a little time for the diversion to work because it only took about four or five minutes to drive from Walnut Creek to Lafayette. We didn't have a police scanner to listen to the police radio calls, but I'd used those handy devices on a few heists before. Instead, we had something just as reliable. Right across the street from our jewelry store was Denny's restaurant, with a local patrol car parked in the lot. I could actually see through the restaurant's windows the two officers sitting at the counter eating. It wasn't more than five minutes after our return from setting up the diversion that these two cops came out of Denny's in a flurry of activity. They jumped into the police cruiser, turned on the emergency lights, and made a few "whoop whoop" sounds with the siren as they peeled out of the restaurant's parking lot.

Dwayne and I just smiled at each other and slowly cruised into a ramming position behind the jewelry store. We quickly rigged up the railroad tie, leaving about four feet sticking out from the car. Crude but effective as hell. I took to the back door of the jewelry store with just three hits using our battering ram. We were in. Dwayne was already inside with the dolly as I turned the car around and backed it up until the back bumper touched the building. I popped open the trunk and went inside to help Dwayne with the safe. By the time I caught up with Dwayne inside the store, at least two minutes had gone by. We had maybe three to four minutes to either get the safe or get away safely.

It was a damn good thing Dwayne was here for the heist because when I made it to help him with the safe, we both discovered just how heavy that bastard was. We struggled just to tilt it onto the dolly. The safe itself was only about four feet high and three feet wide, but it felt like a boat anchor.

We were just about in position to get up to speed with the safe on the dolly when I heard the alarm system kick into another gear. I looked at Dwayne through my ski mask and said we only had one shot at this. With that, Dwayne got nasty. That safe friggin' cleared the back stairs and landed inside the trunk so hard I thought it might make its way into the back seats of the car! Friggin' Dwayne was a beast!

I ran around to where the railroad tie was still attached to the front fender of the car, and with my buck knife, I cut the rope and let it drop to the ground. Dwayne smashed the trunk lid closed, and we jumped into the stolen Caprice. One very large problem was immediately noticeable. The weight of the safe almost had the front wheels of the car off the ground. The car looked like it was doing a wheelie. There was no time for adjustments. We had to get out of the immediate area.

We made it onto westbound Highway 24, but the back bumper was scraping the ground, shooting sparks out. The faster we went, the more fireworks appeared out of the back of the car. Plus, there was very little traction with the front wheels, making it impossible to steer.

I had to pull over. We made it to a pullout on the shoulder of Highway 24, right before the Caldecott Tunnel. We were still in the city limits of Lafayette, and we had to do something fast or abandon ship. Dwayne told me to move. We were right next to a pile of small boulders. Right away, I knew what he wanted to do. We started tossing boulders the size of basketballs into the front seat of the Caprice, except for the little space I needed to drive. We loaded up the front seat with about six or seven hundred pounds of boulders. There wasn't even room for Dwayne. He had to climb into the back seat. It did the trick. We made it out of the area and all the way to my old pal's machine shop for safe-cracking detail. When we pulled up to my pal's shop to use the drill press, once again, he came outside to let us in. It was two hours later before he stopped laughing at us and the Chevy Caprice. Never has a Chevy Caprice worked so hard.

We could have done a commercial on the durability of the Caprice, but we didn't. It took us a lot of extra time and drill bits to crack this safe. We had to drill two extra holes to reach all the loot inside. It took a total of eight hours. This safe had a few shelves inside, making it impossible to reach all the goods with just the extra holes we had to drill. After everything was said and done, the loot was fenced, my machine shop buddy was taken care of, and Dwayne's and my take was over twelve thousand dollars apiece.

I would be lying if I said I wasn't a little worried about Dwayne running off with more than twelve thousand dollars in his pocket. Even though I didn't care much for dope shooters, I did like Dwayne. A few years later, my friend Dwayne would lose his life to the dope monkey that always haunted him. My younger brother John, now a Novato City police officer, was present at Dwayne's autopsy. John told me it was ugly. I often think of Dwayne. I'm not one to dwell on a wasted life. If I were, I would have jumped from the fifth tier inside San Quentin years ago.

CHAPTER 15

Locked Up, Loaded, and Ready to Run

I was still renting the same dive apartment in San Rafael, partying way too much, making it to as many motorcycle events as I could on my old Harley, and pulling a few low-budget heists here and there for rent money. It was the summer of 1988. Even though it wasn't the felony season, I was in need of a good heist. I had to stop taking the same chances with smaller heists and get serious.

The big heist I was looking for found me. I was sitting at home in my apartment in San Rafael when an old crook I knew from Sonoma County called. His name was Bobby-S. Bobby-S told me he was being held hostage in San Francisco at a residential drug program called Delancey Street. Bobby-S and I had known each other for years. We had met while doing juvenile time at the California Youth Authority. He was a couple of years older than me, but every year of his life was dedicated to crime, which was the reason for Bobby-S's phone call. He had gotten my number from some woman we both knew. He told me he was planning to escape from the Delancey Street program that night because he had inside information on a very lucrative heist. Would I be interested? Of course, I said yes and asked what time he would be going over the wall!

The Delancey Street program was not a lockdown facility. It was an alternative drug program instead of a prison sentence, and by going over the wall, Bobby-S would be sealing another trip to the big house.

I picked up Bobby-S on the corner of Park Presidio Avenue and Geary Boulevard in the Richmond district of San Francisco. Two problems met my car that night. First, Bobby-S was wanted by the law by the time he climbed into the passenger seat of my Chevy Camaro. Second, Bobby-S was a serious heroin addict. Before I picked him up, I told myself to quickly do the heist and then get the hell away from him.

After I picked him up, I started grilling him for details on the heist that had him so fired up he was willing to jump ship on a program that had saved his dope-fiend ass from another prison term. He wasn't able to give me much info over the phone, so the whole way to pick him up in the city, I had time to think about how unreliable dope fiends are in these situations—or hell, any situation. But here I was, aiding and abetting another ex-convict.

So, we're headed north out of San Francisco on Highway 101, and he starts to give me the details of this big heist. He says there's a police storage container out by the Sonoma County airport on the property of the county's Honor Farm lock-up. Right away, I said, "Fuck you! Get out!" He starts laughing and says, "Take it easy, Tyke. It's not like it sounds." I said, "Bullshit! I'm not breaking into a jail." He said the storage locker was only a shipping container on the grounds of the lock-up facility, not inside it. He said it was just a steel, padlocked cargo container outside the facility's fences. I didn't like the sound of any of it. Sure, as hell, no matter where the cargo container was, there would be plenty of cops around.

Then Bobby-S hit me with a request to cruise by this place first, which in dope-fiend language means he wanted to get high first. This was not a good start. He said, "I don't want to get high; there's a guy there who knows more about the heist," which in more dope-fiend language means, "I really, really want to get high." We cruised by the place, against every feeling in my body, and I was right—a dope house is where I found myself. So, Bobby did what he needed to do, and we got what info we could from Bobby-S's dope-fiend friend. Then this clown thought he was coming with us on the robbery. This clown could barely stand; he was so blasted on heroin.

I looked at Bobby-S and said, "Either you knock him out, or I'm gonna." Bobby-S put the clown back on his couch, and we split. The cargo container was where everybody said it was, but we still didn't know what was inside of it. Sure enough, police cars were everywhere. We were on foot at this point, on the other side of the airport, looking through my binoculars at the container. Our approach was the problem. There was simply no way to sneak up on this lockup facility. We were going to have to cross the two airport runways, hopefully undetected. It was a small airport with very little traffic after dark. We took our time crossing the airport runways. I wanted to make sure we weren't seen and really didn't want to get hit by a plane. As I got closer to the cargo container, I could see it through my binoculars a lot better. The honor farm lockup facility was right next to the container, but it looked like we could still get to it; there was still a lot of foot traffic around the parking lot. To get to the container, we had to go right through the parking lot.

After we made it completely across the airport runways, we found a spot where we could wait to make our move on the container. We were holed up in a dry drainage ditch, and from there, I could make out the battlefield much better. The majority of the parking lot's police cruisers looked like they were being stored on the property. An hour went by, and the foot traffic in the parking lot was non-existent. I had to slap Bobby-S—just short of an all-out punch—to bring him around and tell him it was time. "Fuckin' heroin, fuck! I should have left him in that ditch." Anyway, we had bolt cutters and a flashlight. From what I could see through my binoculars, I was sure my bolt cutters could handle the padlock on the door, but I was still too far away to see if the cargo container was alarmed. So, here I am, making my way past a county lockup facility to rob an evidence container protected by the secure grounds of county property, with a strung-out heroin addict, when just six hours before I was sitting in my apartment, in my pajamas, eating ice cream and watching "Hogan's Heroes" reruns.

We made it safely to the container, and Bobby-S started saying something about how we had to cut his dope fiend friend in on the loot. I said, "Shut the fuck up." Right on the other side of the container was an auto garage where a few workers were still moving around, working on police cruisers. We don't even know if there is any loot, and Bobby-S wants to argue about the split. I cut the padlock with the bolt cutters.

One quick look around the outside of the cargo container, and I didn't see any visible alarms, but that didn't mean there wasn't one. Right where we were standing, out in the open, alarm or not, we weren't staying long. So, I swung open the latch on the door, and we quietly went inside, closing the cargo container door behind us. We had to be quick, no question about it—get in and get out.

I turned on my flashlight. With the door closed behind us, we were in pitch darkness. It took a few seconds for my eyes to adjust to the flashlight's light. One whole wall was lined with shotguns and all sorts of rifles. I could smell marijuana as soon as I started to breathe again. There were boxes and shelves down the opposite side of the wall of rifles. Bobby-S started grabbing shotguns and making a lot of noise while doing it. I almost lost it with him; I grabbed him by the neck, and he looked at me wide-eyed. I shook my head at this idiot and quietly told him to follow me.

We found, in a brand-new sealed plastic trash can, what looked and smelled like high-quality marijuana, all packaged in vacuum-sealed plastic bags. I told Bobby to grab the other side of the trash can because we were leaving. He tried to protest; he wanted a handful of shotguns. I quietly said, "Fuck you, goodbye." He reluctantly grabbed the other side of the trash can, and we headed towards the door.

Two steps from the door, my flashlight caught sight of a shelf full of pistols, revolvers, automatics, and a couple of hand cannons that looked pretty wild. I quickly scooped all of them into the trash can we were carrying—twenty-five pistols in all. On the same shelf with the pistols was an identical padlock that I had cut with the bolt cutters to gain entry. I peeked out the container's door and saw no movement. We slipped out the door.

I grabbed the bolt cutters and the cut padlock, tossed them into our trash can, and relocked the container door with the identical padlock I found inside. We made good time across the parking lot and back to the drainage ditch where I should have left this idiot dope fiend. We stopped to make sure we hadn't been seen. We were good to go. With the new padlock in place, we had this heist handled, but we still had to make our way back across the two runways of the Sonoma

County airport. We looked both ways before crossing because getting hit by a landing or taking off Lear's jet would definitely hurt. We made it across safely.

We got back to my Camaro, and I took out one of the vacuum-packaged bags of marijuana. I quickly opened it and was hit with the unmistakable smell of powerful, green, sticky marijuana. I had already thrown the rest of the pot into the trunk of the car along with the pistols. I looked at Bobby-S after discovering the quality of the pot and told him that if the rest of the marijuana was the same quality, we did really well money-wise.

This idiot still didn't get it. This kind of marijuana was going for at least three thousand dollars a pound. I didn't know how much more we had in the trunk, but I was going to find out. I knew of a good secluded place nearby where we could determine exactly what we had. I drove at the speed limit the whole way there. We made it to the property of an old chicken ranch that I knew was abandoned. I didn't have a scale to get the exact weight, but my experienced eye and the article in the next day's Sonoma County newspaper, The Press Democrat, reported that the heist's take was twenty pounds of very high-grade marijuana. I gave Bobby-S his half of the pot and eagerly dropped him off at the dope house. There was no way I was going to give him any of the pistols. I told him I had a buyer for all the guns. He begged me for just one pistol. I kicked him out of the car and drove off, feeling really good about it.

Two days later, Bobby-S called me to collect from Sonoma County Jail, asking me to send him some money for coffee and cigarettes. He had been arrested for trying to sell his half of the marijuana to an undercover cop. The Sonoma County police were in full-on bust mode, cracking down on everyone involved with the stolen pistols. They didn't seem to care much about the pot, and luckily, I hadn't given Bobby-S any guns. That idiot would have definitely been caught with them.

The cops didn't link Bobby-S and the marijuana with the cargo container heist. I was even more surprised that dope fiend Bobby-S didn't cut a deal for some sort of leniency. Still, after I sent him a hundred dollars for coffee and cigarettes, I thought a little road trip couldn't hurt. I don't know where Bobby-S is today, but I have a pretty good idea. I sold the marijuana for a good price to a dealer I knew. I got over twenty-four thousand dollars for the pot and unloaded the pistols to some wannabe wise guys in the North Beach district of San Francisco.

My girl Dish had long been out of school and moved down to Orange County, California. Her mom and dad had split, and her mother was also living in Southern California. Dish had started an interior decorating business with another lady, and they were doing well. I jumped onto Interstate Five and pointed my Camaro south. I didn't know what Dish's social life was like at the time, but she was way too pretty to be alone for too long anyway.

I made it to Los Angeles and decided to call her. She answered and quickly lied to me, saying she wasn't seeing anyone at the time. Bless her heart. I didn't care; it was just great to see her. We got a room at a fantastic hotel right on the beach in San Clemente, California. The Tropicana Hotel had themed rooms designed to resemble grass huts on an island. We had a balcony with an ocean view, and for four days, all we had on was the radio. We hadn't been together for a while. On the fifth day, we got dressed, went out, and spent some time together in the world. We had dinner in the Gaslamp District of San Diego. I love downtown San Diego. We spent a couple more days together and said goodbye with a promise to get together again soon. That girl had me and still does! It broke my heart that it turned out to be over nine years before I could hold Dish again.

CHAPTER 16

A Sign I Should've Seen

In the fall of 1988, I got pinched for a heist in Mill Valley, California, which would eventually lead to my third prison sentence, but not before I jumped a few state lines and became a seriously wanted fugitive. Here's what happened: I was once again on a recon and research mission for the lifelong quest of the ultimate heist. I was up above the town of Mill Valley, on Mount Tamalpais, driving through one of the more affluent neighborhoods in the area. I noticed, at a beautiful estate, all the signs that tell a crook, "Over here. This place is robbable!" This was a very attractive three-story estate overlooking the entire North Bay area. I parked my Camaro a few blocks away on a dead-end street and made my way on foot back to this ripe-for-the-picking estate. Surely, a place this nice had a high-dollar alarm system. But as I've said before, a decent alarm system is what you look for in a heist of this nature, giving the owners a false sense of security. I had a problem, though. I was about seven to eight miles up the mountain. The only road up or down was a two-lane road ? called Panoramic Drive, which meant one way up and one way down.

If I were to hit and run the place as planned, I would need to pass the police coming up the mountain as they responded to the alarm. So, what precautions did I take? None. I went ahead with the heist as planned. Even though the place was a bit secluded, with plenty of trees and rough hillside terrain, it was still broad daylight. I conducted a quick recon of the property; I had to be fast with this robbery because I still needed to get off the mountain. I approached the front porch, coming around the estate from the back. The estate was large, sitting on about three acres. I could see that the alarm was indeed active. I pounded on the front door and listened for movement—nothing. With everything I had, I kicked the front door handle. The door gave way, and with the deadbolt locked in place, I split another wooden threshold that did not belong to me. The door swung open violently. I was in. Immediately, I heard the buzzing of the alarm system, signaling that I was involved in another felony. I made my way toward the master bedroom with adrenaline surging. The jewelry box was my destination. I was moving at full speed, about to burst through the two double doors leading to the master bedroom, when I heard a woman's voice from behind the doors. The voice said, "Who's there?" I stopped abruptly but almost went through the double doors anyway. I caught myself just in time. Damn it! I doubled back immediately, and as I was taking the stairs two at a time, the only thing going through my mind was how I was going to safely get off this mountain. I made it back to my Camaro with the speed of an Olympic downhill skier, but I was still far from safe. I knew if I drove down the mountain now, I would most certainly cross paths with the law. Or I could just hide out on the mountain for the day.

As I was thinking this decision over, for maybe twenty seconds, I looked out at the view from where I was standing and, damn it! I had a perfect view of San Quentin prison staring right back at me. I should have taken this as a sign, but I didn't. I jumped in the Camaro, fired it up, and headed down the mountain. Panoramic Drive was a winding mountain road with speeds topping no more than forty miles per hour. By the time I had traveled about half the distance I needed to be out of danger, I passed two Marin County sheriff patrol cars with their lights on, responding to the alarm. I was rounding a sharp turn at the time. My speed was no more than twenty-five miles per hour when the first patrol car passed me going up the mountain. The officer driving the patrol car eyed me like I was having a steak dinner, and the officer right behind him did the same. I knew without a doubt they had identified me as the cause of the silent alarm right then and there. I made a series of quick turns and abandoned my Camaro and my life as I knew it. Sound familiar? Anyway, even though the mountain offered all kinds of escape possibilities, I couldn't shake the sinking feeling that I had been made by the cops. By now, they were all over my Camaro, tracking me via the license plates. With my past history, I was sure to be locked in as their prime suspect. My dive apartment would be surrounded in minutes, and my parole officer would be notified. I even thought about my favorite district attorney, Kit Mitchell—when she got word of this mess, I was sure she would want a piece of me, and certainly not the fun kind. But my immediate problem was getting off this mountain. I made my way cross-country through properties, hillsides, creek beds, and backyards. I thought I had put enough distance between me and the responding police, but every time I tried to come up for air and make a break for it, I would run into another patrol car and have to make another escape back into the wilderness.

I managed to take cover and rest a bit inside an old barn. I found an old work shirt and changed. The barn also had a bicycle that I jumped on and took off, but just when I thought I had avoided handcuffs for the time being, an unmarked police car's front bumper sent me and my bicycle flying into a creek bed. I landed on a couple of boulders the size of Volkswagens that didn't give much when I hit them. Within a minute, I had a dozen police service pistols pointed at me. As I lay there, where I had landed, I believed I was truly hurt, but that didn't matter. I had three sets of handcuffs put on me as I was booked into Marin County Jail.

Charges weren't filed against me right away, but given my parole status, I was chained up and transferred over to San Quentin prison for a parole violation. I was given an eight-month sentence for the violation. On state parole, it's not necessary to be found guilty in a court of law. A parolee essentially has no rights. If the parolee is suspected of criminal activity, the parole department can do what they want with them. So here I was, on an eight-month parole violation, sitting in San Quentin prison, looking up at the mountain where, just days earlier, I had been running from the law.

San Quentin had changed quite a lot since my last stay. The prison itself was no longer maximum security; its status had dropped to medium security, with the exception of death row, which remained maximum security. The prison had also become a reception center, meaning that convicts from Northern California, sentenced to prison, no longer went straight to Vacaville for evaluation. Instead, San Quentin had become the place for evaluation. I'm sure Rick would have hated the changes to San Quentin, as did most of the lifers I talked to who were still there on the main line.

The San Quentin baseball team had changed their name from the Pirates to the Giants and even wore the same uniforms as the San Francisco Giants. Now, I've been a San Francisco Giants fan all my life, but the San Quentin Pirates had a much better ring to it. Rick would have hated that change as well.

Anyway, a couple of months went by, and the stress I was experiencing about whether or not Marin County's District Attorney's office would file charges had subsided a bit. But no such luck for me. Two months before my eight-month parole violation was to expire, I was chained up and transported to Marin County Superior Court. I was housed in maximum security at the Marin jail and charged with first-degree robbery. With my prior record, I was facing up to fifteen or sixteen years in prison. I was dragged down to court the next day for my arraignment hearing and given a copy of the charges against me. The Public Defender's office was appointed to defend me, and I was led away with a court date in three weeks.

The evidence against me, although circumstantial and given my history, still looked strong for a conviction. Also, with Kit Mitchell in charge of my case, a deal before trial seemed hopeless. Kit wanted to have me thrown under the bus, as always. Apparently, I still hadn't grown on her— something about that woman. Despite my situation, my spirits were up, both from seeing Kit again and from the fact that the old avenue of smuggling pot into the Marin County jail remained untouched. So, before long, some other career criminals and I were at least smoking weed, having some laughs, and witnessing more of God's miracles in my life. After two months at Marin County jail, my eight-month parole violation expired. This meant that the state parole hold on me was lifted, making me eligible to post bail.

I kept this information to myself the whole time I was in jail because my bail amount was only five thousand dollars. The District Attorney's office had never thought to ask the judge to raise the amount, mistakenly believing that the state parole hold would never be lifted. It went unnoticed by the authorities right up until the parole hold was lifted. The very same night, I made a few calls, made bail, and ran like hell! I wasn't due back in court for about another week. As soon as my girl in the DA's office found out that I had made bail, Ms. Kit would have flipped out big time! She would not have rested until she convinced the judge to raise my bail to an unreachable amount, so I saw absolutely no reason to stick around for that nonsense.

I visited with my family for a day, not exactly sure of my plans yet, but a road trip was definitely on the agenda. I spent a nice dinner at my mom's, not disclosing any of my troubles, and said goodbye with a hollow promise of good intentions. I wasn't wanted at the time, but since there was no way, I was going to make my next court appearance, the rule "anything goes when you're on the run," as far as I was concerned, applied now.

First off, I was in need of a little traveling money. I knew of a jewelry store over in the East Bay, near San Ramon, in a very affluent neighborhood called Blackhawk. I had done a little reconnaissance a couple of years back and came across this jewelry store by accident. The display cases had some very expensive merchandise. My plan was to walk in wearing some serious running shoes, with some sort of disguise, smash open the finest display case the store had to offer, help myself to the goods, and then break the land speed record.

The store was perfectly situated for such a quick heist. It was at the end of a line of stores in a small strip mall, which would allow me to disappear from view very quickly. I started around noon from downtown San Francisco. I stole a nice mountain bicycle, bought a bushy fake beard from a wig store on Market Street, and with my San Francisco Giants hat on, I jumped on the Bay Area Rapid Transit (BART) train. I took the train all the way out to Dublin, CA. After I departed the train in Dublin, I was able to easily ride the nine to ten miles out to Blackhawk.

Sure enough, the jewelry store was still in business and no doubt still milking the rich folks of Blackhawk. With about an hour until darkness fell, the time was right. I went over my escape route and stashed my mountain bike along the route.

CHAPTER 17

One Job Leads to Another

On my way back to the store for the heist, I stopped at a phone booth and made a quick 911 call saying, "Gunfire at the Dublin train station," and hung up. I know what you are thinking—What a risky move! Well, anything goes, right? I jogged the rest of the way back to the store. I was now in the parking lot, maybe fifty yards from the front glass doors. I could make out about three or four customers and maybe the same number of employees inside the place. It was dark as I made my approach. I was wearing fake beard gloves and had a ball peen hammer up my shirt sleeve. I pulled my San Francisco Giants hat down low as I reached to push open the jewelry store's front door.

I am not sure if I smashed open the best display counter the store had to offer, but with my head down the whole time, not wanting to give the camera a good view, I helped myself to the first counter I encountered. I smashed the top of the display case with one huge swing of the hammer. I had wiped the hammer clean of prints, so I just dropped it. With both hands, I grabbed as much merchandise as I could and then got out of there. In what I thought was record speed, I made it to my mountain bike with no one in pursuit. I pocketed the loot, changed my clothes, trashed the fake beard, and said a small prayer as I threw away my San Francisco Giants hat.

I had about a thirty-minute bicycle ride back to the Dublin train station. Damn it, if I did not see at least eight police cruisers racing from that direction, lights flashing, heading where I had just come from. I made it to the Dublin main station safely and took the train back to San Francisco. The train was crowded, so I was not able to gauge the situation. I got off at the Powell Street station in downtown San Francisco, rode the mountain bike to an apartment complex off McAllister Street, and returned the stolen bike to the same garage I had taken it from seven hours earlier. Strangely, I felt pretty good about that. I know I am still a risk-taker!

I checked into a dive motel off Market Street and, with a bottle of rum beside me, fell asleep watching reruns of "The Untouchables." I stayed in San Francisco for a couple of nights because my "fence" for unloading the jewelry was the same wise guy down in the North Beach district where I used to deal with pot and pistols. The Blackhawk jewelry store heist was very lucrative for such a smash-and-grab job. I had a gold brooch with two one-carat stones of very nice quality set in it, three one-carat diamond wedding rings, and a platinum necklace with a two-carat diamond, along with a lot of smaller pieces. I made over 14,000 in cash. I had some traveling money but no definite plans.

But as fate would have it, while I was at my wise guy buddy's place fencing the jewelry, I ran into a cocaine dealer I knew from Marin County. His name was Vichy, and I knew him well. Vichy had made a killing in the cocaine business back in the 1980s. I had even sold him some cocaine that I had obtained from other dealers. Like I said, we knew each other well. Vichy and his partner Pedro were at my wise guy buddy's place, selling him some good-quality marijuana. Vichy had moved into the pot-growing business, and Pedro was his partner. It turns out Pedro was the actual hands-on grower, and Vichy was the money behind the business. Anyway, Vichy was also there to enlist my wise guy buddy's help because two months prior, Vichy and Pedro had been robbed of over one hundred pounds of marijuana. Vichy wanted to hire my wise guy friend to help him take revenge and recover any product from the people responsible for the robbery. My wise guy friend said he could not help, which surprised me because that was what he did for a living.

I found out later why my Italian friend turned Vichy down. Just as quickly as he said no to Vichy, he said, "Tyke can help you with that problem." Even though I now had a pocket full of traveling money, I would officially be a fugitive again as of Tuesday of the following week, so I listened to what Vichy and Pedro had to say. Over the past couple of years, they had been growing marijuana out in the Midwest, in Pedro's home state of Kansas. They would grow their product there during the summer months, package it up at the end of the year, and move it to California to sell. This year, they had been set up to be robbed by a trusted friend of Vichy's. This friend had arranged a sale of one hundred pounds of pot but then betrayed Vichy and had a crew ready to rob them. Vichy had all the names and information, and I realized then why my wise guy buddy turned Vichy down. The problem was that the wise guy and I both knew and liked the crew that robbed Vichy and Pedro. Hell, I had even worked with a couple of them on jobs.

I told Vichy I could not help him with the crew that did the robbing, but I could definitely help him with his ex-friend, who had set up the robbery in the first place. This ex-friend, whom Vichy had mistakenly trusted, owned a brake and muffler shop in North Marin County. I got a .357 revolver from my wise guy pal and went to see Vichy's ex-buddy at his place of business. At first, he acted cocky and said nothing. I shot three rounds into the ground next to his feet, and he quickly gave up everything. I did not even ask him who did the actual robbery because I already knew, but he provided all their names anyway. He would not stop talking. I got back about fifty pounds of Vichy and Pedro's product, along with some cash. Based on recovering some of their product, I earned a job offer in Vichy and Pedro's marijuana-growing business out in Kansas.

It just so happens I was looking for some travel plans. So, two days after a felony warrant was issued for my arrest due to a failure to appear in court, Vichy's younger brother and I loaded up a U-Haul van full of halide lights, shades, ballast, and all kinds of hydroponic indoor growing equipment and headed east. I was now in the marijuana growing business, which was a career close to my heart. I loved smoking pot. A plan was developing in my mind as

Vichy's older brother, and I drove east. This is what it was: spend a couple of years out in the Midwest growing pot with these guys, make some good money, come back to Marin County, and retain a good lawyer to arrange a surrender along with a guilty plea in the pending Mill Valley case for a reasonable amount of prison time. Sound good? Well, it did back then, but a whole lot of different things happened out there in Kansas. Here is how it went:

The home base of the Kansas growing operation was in a nice two-bedroom house just north of Manhattan, Kansas, at least four or five miles from the closest neighborhood. It was perfect for a wanted ex-convict from California—that would be me. The house provided for every need: a satellite dish to catch the Giants and the Forty-Niners games, a complete weight room, and the house itself had a great view of a reservoir called Tuttle Creek that provided great fishing. I could not have been more dialed into a better situation as a fugitive, plus I was employed.

The house itself was set up perfectly. There was a large basement for the winter indoor growing season and a one-hundred-and-fifty-gallon propane gas tank to run the electricity needed for the grow lights. I arrived in Kansas in the winter of 1988, so it was the indoor growing season. Not only did we grow retail pots indoors, but we also grew what were called "Mother plants." What we would do with these plants is, one month before we could start growing outdoors, cut little "top cuttings" off the mother plants and transplant them into the soil, like peat moss, and treat them with rooting solution until they took root. Around the end of April, we would transplant them one more time to pre-dug holes outside with an all-purpose potting soil. The main reason for this process was that the plant was already a proven female plant. You do not want male marijuana plants—just one male plant can pollinate your entire crop, and you end up with seedy weed. No good! The value of your pot drops drastically. These marijuana plant clippings, known as "clones," when fully grown, will produce more marijuana per plant than your traditional Christmas tree-looking seedling. These clones would grow in the shape of a large bush, but I am getting ahead of myself. We were not outdoors yet. I was in Kansas just a couple of months and still tending to the indoor growing, and it was the holiday season. The holidays in Kansas were lonely for me. It's hands down my favorite time of the year, but I was a fugitive, and with Vichy and Pedro out of town, as they usually were, someone had to tend to the indoor growing. I didn't mind that much. I was in the woods with guns, two dogs, and an indoor pot operation.

As usual with me, I was away from my family, and I missed them. I had a dirt motorcycle way out there with me to get back and forth to the store for supplies, so I was okay for now. I called a few friends and my mom from time to time. I even made a call to my old lawyer, a public defender back at the Marin County Civic Center. She was a good lawyer and a very thoughtful person. Her name was Terry Zimmerman, and she was very easy on the eyes. Anyway, when I finally got her on the phone, I had to try her a couple of times as public defenders are super busy. She was so nice. She talked in a low voice as if someone was listening. I got a kick out of her. But what she had to say wasn't so good. She said my girl Kit Mitchell had blown up at anyone who would listen. But in the end, it was the District Attorney's mistake not to see the parole hold being lifted once the violation expired, and Terry said that just made Kit even more twisted. I told Terry that I could just picture Kit goose-stepping around the courtroom in her Gestapo high heels. Terry laughed until we said goodbye. I knew I would have a battle when I got back home, and it sure looked like it would be ugly. The winter's indoor grow season was a success, but the real money was to be made outdoors. With marijuana plants, nothing produces like the sun. The most powerful indoor grow lights are only a fraction compared to the sun. Our outdoor growing spot was a two-hour drive to the west.

Once the plants had grown to three or four feet high, we were going to have to move out to western Kansas and live with the plants. What I meant was that I, Vichy and Pedro would only fly in from California about twice a month for a day or two. They were there just long enough to guide me in a few directions with the growing. They had me tending to the plants twenty-four hours a day, so there was no need for them to stick around. Plus, they both had other illegal activities going on. Vichy was still dealing in cocaine and heroin, and Pedro had a pretty girl he was strung out on. Something troubling had been happening that threatened everything. I wasn't aware of it until I got out to Kansas. Vichy had developed a heroin habit, and I had never known anyone successful on that shit. But he stayed away enough. Besides, it was Pedro who was the pot-growing genius. He knew everything about growing quality marijuana, and I learned a lot about it myself with Pedro's guidance. So, all I needed was for Pedro to show up every couple of weeks to check up on me. Well, the clones we took from the mother pot plants had been in the ground, out in western Kansas, for about two months now. It was time for me to move out there for the plants would soon need everyday attention. The outdoor growing operation was perfect. Pedro had used this same spot for the past three years.

It was a dry creek bed running in between miles of Alfalfa fields. We had a well and from the well ran about two miles of PVC pipe along the bottom of the dry creek bed. The creek bed was lined with huge Bay trees that stayed green all year long, and at every little opening of these trees, I had twenty to thirty pot plants growing strong. A little over nine hundred plants in all. With nine hundred plants in the ground, if I made sure they never wanted for anything until late September, we should easily clear five hundred pounds of clean packaged pot for sale and I was in for a third. I was looking at a little over two hundred thousand dollars for my end. Sounds good, huh? Well, we had a dust storm in late July that beat the shit out of more than half the crop, So the profits of my first outdoor growing operation took a severe beating. This friggin' dust storm was like nothing I'd ever been through. It lasted for more than five hours, well after dark. I was running around the creek bed all night trying, frantically to tie the pot plants' branches down. But with this dust storm, I couldn't see at all. It was miserable. I wasn't even able to tally up the damage until the daybreak. I felt and looked like Ol'

Henry Fonda in the movie, "The Grapes of Wrath." Anyway, the final count of the damage was heartbreaking. We lost over five hundred plants but made more than enough to finance another season so I was staying one more year. Once September showed up, we had three hundred and ninety full-grown, fully budding marijuana plants. We harvested in late September, and the manicuring would take another month. Manicuring is a process of separating the water leaves of the pot plant from the premium product, which is the marijuana flower bud. Manicuring is done with scissors and can be time-consuming. So, just before Halloween, we had two hundred and sixty pounds of high-grade marijuana for sale.

One more problem remained. We had to transport the marijuana back to California because that's where the buyers were. We rigged up a pickup truck with a false gas tank that I thought was pretty cool. It was a 1. shaped diesel gas tank mounted in the back bed of the pick-up with a toolbox mounted over the top. The 1-shaped diesel tank had a false bottom. Inside the tank's spout and breather, we mounted a couple of capped-off pipes with real diesel fuel inside the capped-off pipes. So, if anyone should open up the tank, they would find diesel fuel inside. But another problem popped up. The false bottom diesel tank would only hold two hundred and ten pounds inside. It wouldn't fit even one more pound even after we vacuum-packed every package. The trouble was you really didn't want to compact the marijuana that much because that takes away from the whole presentation when trying to see the product. When selling marijuana, especially selling a lot of marijuana, looks are a lot of what sells it for a good price or not. So, with way more pot on hand for our own personal use, the problem with getting the other fifty pounds out to market in California was solved by me.

We vacuumed and sealed the fifty pounds of pot that wouldn't fit into the diesel gas tank one more time, giving each of the fifty pounds a double vacuum seal. I boarded a Grey Hound bus with two locked duffle bags containing the pot in Topeka, Kansas. I rode the bus to Denver, Colorado, where I took a compartment on an Amtrak train and rode all the way to Oakland, California. Being wanted like I was, I couldn't drive the pick-up truck anyway, but with this being pre-Bin-Laden days, I was perfect for a bus and train: I love traveling by train. I spent most of the trip inside the bar car.

CHAPTER 18

The Heroin Problem

It was just about winter time and blasting through the Rocky Mountains inside the bar car was big fun. I met a pretty lady, who I still think about sometimes, and we smiled the entire trip. I was looking forward to seeing California since deciding to stay another year out in Kansas. Vichy picked me up at the train station in Oakland. I had lipstick marks on my face, and Vichy laughed all the way to Marin County. Since I was still a fugitive, I had to lay low, but I managed to see my mom and dad plus squeeze in a little partying. I tried to reach Dish, but she was still down in southern California and I was only staying for a day or two. We managed to sell all the marijuana except ten pounds. Vichy said he would stay behind and deal with it. Pedro and I boarded a United airline flight, and we flew first class to Kansas City. We decided we could use a vacation. We went on a fishing trip to Branson, Missouri. We went fishing at Table Rock Lake and took in a few shows in the city of Branson. It was comfortable. We rented a cabin right on the lake, and, the greedy bastard that I am, I caught way over my limit of trout every day we were there. Vichy was still out in California mainly because he couldn't score heroin in Kansas. Vichy's heroin use worried both me and Pedro, but what harm could he be to us if he stayed out in California? So, Pedro and I got our shit together for the indoor growing season. Pedro and I were doing great with the indoor winter growing of the mother plant when Pedro got a phone call from the land owner of the Alfalfa fields where we grew outdoors in the creek bed. So, Pedro drives out to western Kansas and returns the next day, all pissed off. The landowner's name was Larry. Anyway, Larry and his wife had just given birth to a baby girl-poor kid. These two drunks had already gone through their share of the money from the previous growing season, and they were blaming Pedro for the friggin' dust storm that cut the profits in half. Pedro told me that he tried to reason with these thick square heads but no go. He said we had to find another outdoor location for our crop this summer. He said with the way Larry's wife Helen was complaining and threatening to call the authorities they could no longer be trusted. So, as the month of April got closer, we still had no decent outdoor spot to plant our crop. With the mother pot plants ripe, we could start cutting the tops and treating them with a rooting solution any day now. Vichy came out for a visit. He looked bad. Heroin-fuck. Vichy already knew about our problem of no outdoor spot, so he suggested the outdoor right there on the Manhattan property.

It was a great location, and Pedro and I had discussed the same idea before. The house and the property were all in Vichy's name, so with Vichy ok with the whole idea, hell, he even thought it was his idea, Pedro and I got to work, and Vichy got himself and his heroin habit back to California. The Manhattan property was perfect for a crop, maybe a total of about five hundred plants. Pedro and I planted seven hundred plants. The property had absolutely no foot traffic and a two-mile single-lane driveway with a locked gate and no trespassing signs posted everywhere. Kansas was full of squares and law-abiding folk. We were in a good spot for growing outdoors. At the beginning of April, Pedro and I planted seven hundred clones in the ground. We were off to a good start. Pedro waved goodbye and went to stay with his girlfriend out in California. Pedro had a lifelong friend living about seven or eight miles down the reservoir shoreline from where I was, so I would go for a visit now and then with the dogs and party with him from time to time. His name was Ben, and other than Ben and some of Ben's friends, it was just me and Pedro's dogs. I love dogs. Always have. I even have a tattoo of my favorite long-gone dog. "Max". Max was a cool person! Anyone who knew him could tell you the same. Max went everywhere with me. Sometimes he went out with me. He was a German shepherd and Collie mix. Great pooch! Pedro's dogs were mutts but good ol'boys. Pedro's friend Ben was also in the marijuana-growing business. He had taken over the creek bed growing operation in western Kansas at "Larry's the drunks" land.

Pedro had warned Ben to be careful that Larry's wife was a witch, but Ben wasn't "hands-on" with the growing part of the operation. He was just financing the deal. Anyway, things at the Manhattan house were smooth for me and the dogs. We were going along well. The plants were thriving in the Kansas summer, and I looked to be well on my way to hiring a decent lawyer back home and maybe wiggling out of some serious trouble. But then shit caved in on me big time. Around the middle of July Pedro came skidding into the front driveway of the Manhattan house around midnight. Out in rural Kansas, you can hear the smallest noises from way off. So, when Pedro skidded to a stop, I was already up for I heard him coming. He jumped out of his truck with the news of Vichy being arrested with the last ten pounds of marijuana and a kilo of cocaine. The dumb ass had checked into a local motel in Marin County and, with all his heroin-addicted brain damage, started riffing out phone calls from the motel room, raising warning flags for the motel phone switchboard who, in turn, called the local police department and Vichy was pinched.

I asked Pedro if we should pull up the stakes and take a loss on a shortened growing season! Pedro said to sit tight. Vichy should be out on bail today or tomorrow. Vichy made bail the next day. Pedro and I talked to him by phone. He said the authorities have no idea about his Kansas ties or property and to stay put and finish the growing season. We hung up on Vichy, not being sure of anything. I told Pedro Vichy is on the heroin crap and isn't thinking clearly. I said we should harvest now and take the loss on the shortened season. Pedro also knew Vichy was an idiot on that heroin crap, but Pedro had a pending cultivation charge that he had been out on bail now for over two years. With Vichy now out on bail, they both needed the cash from the crop I was growing more than ever, I was still over a month from harvest time, and I knew damn well what Pedro and Vichy were thinking. If they swayed safely away for that amount of time, they could cash in on the crop, or if they got raided, either way, they're not here until the plants turn into money or not. I saw it this way.

The house was in Vichy's name, and the cops were on their way here. I was right. The day before we got raided, a plane flew over the property five or six times really low. Pedro was in town getting supplies. When he returned, I told him about the airplane. He said, "Don't sweat it. Planes fly by like that all the time out here." I said, "Bullshit, I've been out here for over a year now, and I've never seen that kind of shit before." Friggin' Pedro was scheduled to leave the next day, so he wasn't sweating anything yet. The next day arrived, and Pedro's plane left Kansas City airport at six pm. He had to run to town to pick up a few things before he left. I had work to do with the plants since it was fertilizing day. I heard Pedro take off in his truck, but no more than a minute later, I heard a lot of other noises. I went around to the front of the house, and there was no mistaking the stomach-turning orders being shouted at poor Pedro. From the house, I could not see the confrontation between the law and Pedro because of the dense cover of trees. Even better, they couldn't see me. It didn't sound like Pedro was going to make a big fight that night. He had run head-on into four Suburban full of drug agents. The dirt driveway was only a one lane one way. You could not pass another vehicle because of a thick grove of trees along the shoulder of the road. I could tell from the noise that Pedro's encounter with the cops was less than a mile away.

It was more than clear that I was not long for staying. I had a no-bail warrant and a parolee-at-large warrant out for me in California-both, very good reasons for not wanting to be introduced to Pedro's new pals. I figured I had maybe two or three minutes. I gathered up some things. I took one last look up the one-lane dirt leading away from the house and saw several agents making their way toward the house on foot with guns drawn. My career criminal ass needed no further persuasion to leave. I ran out the back of the place with two pistols, a grocery bag containing cash, a pot, and a bottle of Bacardi rum. As I said before, the house was pretty well-secluded. Mother Nature had provided plenty of coverage in the way of very thick groves of trees. As I made my way from the house at my traditional match one speed, I had to slow down a bit because, remember what. I said about being able to hear the slightest noise out there in rural Kansas from a long way off. My two-hundred-pound ass blazing a trail would have been heard easily. Plus, I had to stay close to the trees because that low-flying airplane from the day before was back, making tight circles around the property. Even as I made my way through the Kansas countryside, I could still hear all the drug agents having their way with the house from a long way off. I was still a good twenty-five miles from the town of Manhattan. Kansas, so I had no other choice but to make my way to Pedro's home-boy Ben's house.

CHAPTER 19

A Bad Feeling

I made it to Ben's house safely. Ben was super paranoid about the whole raid since Ben was also involved in the marijuana business. Even though he wasn't directly involved with Pedro and Vichy at that time, he had been in the past. The raid on the Manhattan house and the arrest of Pedro was all over the local news that night. It even said that the arrest information came from a drug arrest in California. Friggin' Vichy-heroin fuck! The drug enforcement agents, federal agents, and local cops were all in on the raid. Since Pedro was already out on bail from a marijuana growing arrest over two years before, his bail was set at two hundred and fifty thousand dollars. The law had the marijuana crop estimated at over two million dollars in street value. Fucking cops, there was no such street on the planet. Even if we had sold the crop by doobies, we only would have maybe cleared five or six hundred thousand.

Anyway, I looked at the situation I was screwed. I had one change of clothes, a little cash, and some pot, and I had already drank the rum-all real pirates drink rum. The dogs were with Pedro on his track during the raid. I blamed Vichy for this disaster, although that helped nothing. I never considered myself a genius, but fucking heroin addicts are the worst. You can't talk any sense to them; making sense is the furthest thing from their minds. Well, anyway here I am with my situation looking bleak. My Kansas employment is now shot to shit, wanted in California for what's sure to equal a lengthy prison stay, and my hope to return home with enough cash to hire a decent lawyer to help smooth out my California trouble has been wrecked.

I mentioned that Ben had taken over the creek bed growing operation in western Kansas. He had a grower named Bo out there doing all the hands-on work. Bo was about three weeks from harvest. Ben said he was going to have to hire some help for Bo with harvest and the manicuring of the marijuana. Would I be interested in the job? I had met Bo before, and he was a good enough old boy. Ever since Pedro had his falling out with Larry, the creek bed land owner, I had pictured myself knocking Larry's teeth out the back of his head. My employment prospects were slim, so I took the job against my better judgment. I knew what was in store for me before I even got there. I was going to bite my tongue just to get along with this retard who, a year before, blamed Pedro for the dust storm. Here I was, headed out to western Kansas to help with a pot crop that was going to bring in very much money for me anyway, on the way out there. Ben drove me out there himself. Ben and I were talking, and I expressed my concerns about going back out to Larry's land. Ben said he understood, and he agreed with me that the land owner, Larry, was a piece of shit, but just stick it out because we only had a few more weeks of growing to do out there. We also talked about me growing some crops of marijuana for him the following season, and that sounded good, for I was still in need of some serious lawyer money. Ben had seen the crop I grew at the Manhattan house. He would come by from time to time and liked what he saw.

The Manhattan house crop I grew was going to bring in some serious cash. Friggin' Vichy-heroin fuck! I hated the idea of another year out in Kansas, but I would do it because I needed the money. We arrived out in western Kansas, and Bo knew we were coming. Bo had fixed up the old farmhouse next to the well where the PVC pipe ran from down the length of the creek bed. The old farmhouse was a two-bedroom place that Mother Nature had beaten to hell. The previous year, when I stayed with the plants in the creek bed. I bunked inside a big tent. It was a bit primitive, but the pirate in me didn't mind. I had rigged up an outdoor shower, and I barbequed every day. It was only for the last two months of the growing season when the plants required everyday attention.

Anyway, like I said, Bo had turned the old farmhouse into livable quarters, and it was fine with me because Larry the retard and his wife Helen lived in the main house about two miles away on the other side of their property. Ben dropped me and all our supplies off and went over to see Larry. He told us he would return in three weeks for the harvest. Bo and I settled in. Bo was a good person who was just out to make some money. He didn't like Larry one bit, which, to me, showed good character, and now, with me signed on, Larry pretty much stayed away, which was cool. Bo and I got to work. Bo had done a wonderful job with his crop. He had about nine hundred full-grown clones of sticky green Sinsemilla, which is a lot of work for just one guy to do. I know he didn't get any help from Larry the retard. Now, way out in western Kansas, Saturday nightlife consisted of a trip to the county supermarket. This part of the world was home to sunburned necks, arms, and the Klan. Not that I was in much of a party mode but Bo told me about a bar he would go to about once a week. Get this, the bar he frequented was in the basement of a county courthouse in the middle of the town square in Randolf, Kansas! Bo was aware that I had some unattended trouble out in California, but he assured me this place wasn't what it sounded like, so I said ok. Around ten pm one weekend, we made our way to the town of Randolf in Bo's pick-up truck. We parked out in front of the courthouse in this "turn of the century" town square. There was a line of farm-worn pick-up trucks in front of the courthouse. I thought to myself, "Damn, this place is jumping."

Anyway, even though there were no cops in this basement/bar, I did meet two Klansmen, one judge, and a group of boys that I was positive had not cracked a smile. Since John E. Kennedy held the presidency. They only served whiskey and Pepsi-no ice. These were the sourest group of boys I'd ever encountered, and I'd spent years inside San Quentin prison. From that night on, anytime I found myself in a bad situation, I would say, "Could be worse. I could be in Randolf, Kansas, drinking whiskey and Pepsi in the county courthouse with no ice." I would talk about this night with family and friends years later, but it was definitely something you had to see for yourself to get the full effect. It was truly like stepping back fifty years in time. Bo did not think anything was strange about it. I found out Bo grew up out here in western Kansas. I told him, "Sorry, honest." Anyway, we were a week away from our planned harvest. Ben was due back out here in a few more days to help us with the manicuring and drying process of the marijuana crop.

Bo and I were talking out at the old two-bedroom farmhouse when we heard Larry's truck come skidding to a stop out front. He burst into the place, and it was easy to see that he was shit-faced drunk. He said that he finally kicked the bitch out, meaning his wife, Helen. He said that they had fought big time and that she packed her and the baby's things, and he kicked her out. I knew right then this equaled trouble. I told Bo we should harvest all night long and go manicure the crop at another location, but both of these door-knob idiots said Helen wouldn't go to the cops.

My stomach told me otherwise. I had a good warning system inside my stomach, and it saved me from handcuffs more than once, and I knew the cops were coming. We were unsuccessful at trying to reach Ben that night by telephone, but I still insisted we should harvest now and get gone. These two "Jethros" said let's wait. I should have just split. The next day came, and at about three in the afternoon, I was busy watering the plants in the creek bed one last time before our scheduled harvest when I noticed a helicopter up high overhead just hovering like a dragonfly. I turned the water off and quickly hopped on a quad runner we had and rode through the creek bed for a couple miles toward Larry's house. I made it over to Larry's house, where he and Bo were still trying to get a hold of Ben by phone. I got their attention, and we all stared at the hovering helicopter for more than ten minutes. I watched the helicopter disappear from sight after hovering directly over the top of the creek bed. I was the first to speak. I said, "No question about it. Someone called the cops on us." I might as well have been talking to the pot plants because these two square heads were still in denial of the situation, I was positive about. Then, I made the biggest mistake of my Kansas marijuana-growing career stayed. What I wanted to do, and what I should have done, is knock Larry the retard out, tie him up, and make Bo help me harvest the pot crop through the night.

When Ben finally got word about my plan, he was "gun shooting" mad at Bo and Larry the retard, but when Ben found out everything, it was way too late. Here's what happened: The next morning, cops showed up, and that made me even madder because we really did have all night to harvest and get gone. It was a beautiful fall morning; I remember thinking what could be wrong on a morning like this? Soon, my answer would come. Bo and Larry went to town for nothing but lies because they were too scared to stick around. I had the quad runner all gassed up and ready for any needed escape through the creek bed. The creek bed was my only chance to escape using the cover of the big trees.

The Alfalfa fields on both sides of the creek bed were only about one foot high this time of year, and western Kansas is so friggin' flat you could see forever. I was sitting on the quad runner smoking a doobie down in the creek bed. I heard the helicopter first. It came in low, just above the big Bay trees. It created such a dust cloud that it helped me get out of the immediate area on the quad runner, but I didn't get far.

My plan was to take the creek bed back to Larry's house about two miles away. I was gonna grab Larry's truck and get further out of the area, but I was cut off by armed cops on foot, making their way to the marijuana crop right down the middle of my escape route. They drew down on me with their pistols as soon as we saw each other. They were still about fifty yards from me, so I whipped the quad runner around and made for the way I had just come. The helicopter had me and followed my path the whole way. These cops had their approach planned well. They came from all sides, but they still weren't getting close enough to me.

I was standing up on the footpegs of the quad runner, looking up out of the creek bed, trying to find a spot in between the oncoming swarm of cops that I could slip through when not really watching where I was going. I hit a rock head-on and went ass over the handlebars, and landed surprisingly alive. The quad runner didn't make it. I was able to run, and that's what I did. I got out of the creek bed. I was still under tree cover, but that friggin' helicopter was still right above me. The cops on foot and in vehicles were all converging on the marijuana crop. I was maybe forty yards from the back end of the farmhouse. There was a dirt motorcycle on the side on the side of the farm house that I was going to try to get to. I made a run for it, leaving the cover of the big Bay trees. The helicopter swooped down right next to me, hovering maybe twenty feet off the ground. The helicopter was an old Huey type. They must have had some sort of thermo heat-seeking sensors on board because they knew right where I was even when I was under the cover of the trees.

Anyway, this hovering helicopter was right in my face. Its side sliding door was wide open with a national guardsman manning the fifty-caliber machine gun pointed right at me as if I were Viet Cong in Southeast Asia. It took a minute to sink in that I had been captured by a helicopter. The ten or so drug agents, pointing guns behind me, had a hand in the arrest also. I was handcuffed with about four sets of cuffs and booked into federal custody in Wichita, Kansas. The four federal marshals who transported me all the way back to Wichita all had matching crew cuts. All four of their heads were matching squares. It was eerie as shit. None of them said a word or cracked a smile during the three-hour trip. I thought I was in an episode of the. "Twilight Zone" being driven to another planet. It turns out that I wasn't that far off. I was booked into the federal holding of the Sedgewick County jail in Wichita, Kansas, with nothing but John Deere's finest. Every convict in that jail had a down south, moonshine accent. Their crimes all had something to do with livestock.

I had a one million dollar bail and two no-bail warrants from California. Larry's wife had told the authorities I was some sort of escaped convict out of California, and that story spread all the way to the news report on TV out there in John Deere's world. Helen had squealed on more shit than was even happening. It's pretty common. When someone squeals, they sensationalize the squealing to make it more dramatic. Anyway, Helen gave the cops her husband, Larry, and the grower, Bo. The cops issued warrants for both of them. Larry and Bo both hired lawyers and arranged to surrender to the authorities the next day. They were booked into the federal holding of the Sedgewick County jail in Wichita. They were put into the same cell block as me. I only had a couple hours to tell them both what friggin' idiots I thought they were that we didn't harvest the day before the raid. It was also my fault for listening to them and not leaving. They both made bail a couple hours later. I didn't.

CHAPTER 20

The Art of Survival

I stayed in the Wichita, Kansas, federal holding for a year and a half. My no-bail holds on me from California meant I should get credit for time served in Kansas on whatever was waiting for me in the way of prison time in California. I knew I had a fight waiting for me out there. I could picture my girl Kit Mitchell goose-stepping around the District Attorney's office in her high heels, rubbing her hands together, dreaming of having her way with me. I have to admit it made me kinda hot. I know I am a freak, but something about that chick.

Well, a couple days later, we were all dragged in front of a United States magistrate in federal court. I found out on that first court appearance that modern lock-up procedures had not made their way out to Wichita, Kansas. About an hour before we were to appear in court, these mid-west jail guards put us all into the conference room together and left us alone. My attorney, Larry and Bo, their attorneys, and I were all in this conference room without supervision. I said, "Damn, do they do this with us every court hearing?" My attorney, a really nice lady named Syd Gilman, said, "Yes. They leave us alone in these conference rooms before every court hearing." Everyone was looking at me like I was some dumb ass when it came to the ways of the court procedures. Right away, my criminal mind started to go to work.

Bo and Larry were both out on bail, so there was no doubt in my mind, without even asking, that they were going to want to string the court proceedings way out into the future, and my fate was sealed with the California holds and all. With the marijuana cultivation charge, we were all facing a maximum sentence of five years in federal prison. Right away, I knew what I was going to do. As our lawyers talked, I pulled Bo to the side and told him what I needed him to do. Larry was too stupid. I told Bo, at our next court hearing, to bring me an ounce of good marijuana, but before you bring it to me, clean it of stems of seeds, compact it into a plastic baggie, and then squeeze it into a rubber balloon. Even though the drug cops had confiscated the marijuana from the creek bed, there was still a lot of pot hidden around the farm that Larry's wife didn't know about. Bo. not having any idea at all as to what I was going to do with this ounce of marijuana, said, "Sure, Tyke, no problem. Next court hearing, I'll bring it."

Our next court appearance was two weeks away. The sixth floor of the Sedgewick County jail, where all the federal prisoners were housed. It wasn't the worst place I had ever done time. The jail's exercise yard was on the roof, and the federal prisoners, myself included, had access to the yard all day long, and it was a perfect spot for smoking pot. The next court appearance date arrived, and once again, Bo, Larry, our lawyers, and I were all allowed to be left alone in this conference room just outside of the courtroom. The first time Bo brought me an ounce of pot, it was a straight-up fiasco. First off, I know for sure that Larry, Bo, and all three of our attorneys have never forgotten what I did on that day. Like I said, the first time Bo smuggled me in an ounce of pot was a major fiasco.

Obviously, he had no idea of what I was going to do. We are all locked inside this conference room, and Bo pulls out an ounce of sticky, green, smelly, very high-quality marijuana and hands it to me. Right away, the whole room smells of marijuana. Everyone in the room, at this point. Looks to be in mild panic. Then Bo hands me a balloon the size of a medicine ball. I said, "What the fuck!?" The ounce of pot is all still budded up with stems throughout it all. Instead of telling Bo he was an idiot, I got right to work; Bo already knew he was an idiot anyway. I cleaned the pot of stems as fast as I could and I rolled up the pot as tight as I could inside the plastic sandwich baggie that Bo had brought it in. The friggin' balloon was way too big to be of any use. I emptied my lawyer's soda can and pushed the rubber balloon inside the empty soda can. I wasn't sure if a thrown-away balloon would bring any unwanted attention from the cops out here in Kansas, but it sure would of in California. I crushed the soda can with the balloon inside of it and threw it in the garbage can, hoping it would not be found, and it wasn't. Anyway, I was still packing the ounce of pot inside the sandwich baggie when I noticed some perfume inside my lawyer's purse sitting on the floor between us. I had to do something about the smell of marijuana inside the room.

With my lawyer's permission, I sprayed perfume around the conference room. When I put the perfume back in my lawyer's purse, I noticed some lip gloss that I could also use. Again, with my lawyer's permission. I grabbed the lip gloss. I continued to compact the pot inside the sandwich baggie, and for over twenty minutes, no one except me had said a word inside that conference room. All eyes were on me with no idea what I was going to do. Once again, with my lawyer's permission. I took the perfume out of her purse and took care of the smell one last time. I returned the perfume to her purse, and with dead silence in the room with all interest on me, I took the compacted ounce of marijuana, dabbed a little bit of lip gloss on the outside of it, and with a what the hell smile on my face; I slipped the marijuana package up inside my butt.

Now, right up until that last thirty seconds, no one in that conference room had any idea of what my plan was, but right after those last seconds passed, every single one inside that conference room looked as though they had just experienced some sort of near-death trauma-always makes me giggle a little when I remember back to that time and at how freaked out they all were, just another embarrassing reality of life behind bars. All the other times we were back in that conference room together, after that first fiasco, Bo handled all the packaging instructions smoothly.

Everybody inside the room would usually give me as much privacy as they could. It was so funny. One time, I had them all bunched up in one of the corners of the room with all their backs to me, facing into the corner as if they were all being punished for being bad in school. That was one of the many times I thought to myself, "Damn, I should write a book because no one's gonna believe this shit." Thoughts and situations like this come and go a lot in my life. Anyway, like I said, I stayed in federal custody in Wichita for about a year and a half. Bo, Larry, and I were all sentenced to five years in federal prison. Bo and Larry served their sentence inside a federal prison camp. They didn't have criminal records until then, anyway. I was about to be extradited back to California for jumping bail on that Mill Valley heist, but before that happened, I got word inside the jail that my old partner Pedro, who got pinched at the Manhattan house growing operation, had received a federal prison sentence of twenty-seven years.

You see, after the Manhattan house arrest, Pedro finally got out on a reasonable bail bond, but Pedro was also out on bond from a previous marijuana cultivation charge. It was expensive, but he was free, on bond on both charges, and he ran like hell! You have to love his spirit! He was arrested six months later in a Florida airport with fake identification, trying to leave the county with a bunch of cocaine. Ol' Pedro loved to snort cocaine. Anyway, Pedro got slammed hard. Twenty-seven years inside federal prison meant he would be required to serve eighty-five percent of his sentence before he could be considered for parole. That meant Ol' Pedro had to serve about twenty-three years-Ugly! Pedro is a good man, and even though I had troubles of my own to deal with, I truly felt bad for him.

But as God is truly looking out for us all, I will be able to share some good news about Pedro and the outgoing Clinton administration later on in this story. So, I was chained up and bused to Topeka, Kansas. I boarded "Con Air" with the federal marshal's air transportation service. I was flown out to Travis Air Force Base in Fairfield, California. After a seriously nerve-racking plane ride, these planes the federal marshals use to transport convicts are nothing short of dangerous. It's amazing we haven't heard about these airplanes crashing more than we already do. The friggin' pilots have to be drinking the way we were all over the place. I stopped one of the federal marshals as he was walking in the aisle, and I asked him if we might crash. We were still at thirty-five thousand feet altitude and bouncing all over. He told me that all the airplanes in their fleet are old, retired commercial airliners that the EAA won't officially clear for public use anymore. I said, "Don't talk to me anymore. I don't fly well." Miraculously, we landed safely in Fairfield, California.

I was turned over to the custody of two Marin County sheriffs who came to Travis Air Force Base to take me back to the Marin County jail. They must have had ten pounds of forehead apiece. They were brow-beating me down with their mean, hard looks. It actually looked like they were both in pain. I told them that I met their four square-headed cousins out in Kansas. I told them that they were all doing fine with the federal marshals' haircut squad. They actually looked like they understood me. Ol' 'Kit Mitchell must have handpicked these two herself. Something about that chick. Well, I made it back to familiar surroundings-maximum, security at the Marin County jail. Sure enough, I knew some of the crooks currently housed there. I had brought with me, from Kansas, a little stash of pot. No need to get into how I managed that. I just did. So, after getting stoned and reacquainted with a few of the local hoods, I inquired about any changes in the jail's procedures that may get in the way of my "Old Faithful" avenue of smuggling pot inside.

Things were still the same, so I was good to go with starting the process of obtaining a few extras inside the Marin County lock-up. I was scheduled for court the next morning, just an arraignment hearing to hear the charges against me and to assign the Public Defender's office to my case. I wasn't in California for more than eight hours, and I was the cause of another felony. Smuggling pot into the county lock-up never seemed like a criminal act to me. The results would only be mellow convicts buying food and candy from the jail store and., with my twisted sense of reality, stimulating the local economy. My first court hearing went smoothly. Arraignment hearings, for the most part, are just a formality.

However, I did get my first look at Kit Mitchell in several years. She was wearing a skirt and her regular "come get me" high heels. Ok, Ok, sorry. Anyway, she didn't need to be present at this first court hearing. She was there for only one reason: the status of "No bail" in my case continued to stand. Bless her heart. I was appointed a lawyer who constantly brought me bad news. I nick named him "Dark Cloud" because he did look a bit like an Indian. My pretty warm-hearted attorney, Terry Zimmerman, who I spoke with from Kansas over the phone, had gotten herself married and moved to San Diego. She was a very good person, and I wished her well. I was stuck with "Dark Cloud". He seemed ok, but he was such a "woe is me" kind of dude. It's not a good quality for a defense attorney. I was back in court a couple weeks later, and although I had a mask and gloves on during the Mill Valley heist, circumstantial evidence was my enemy once again. I was seen leaving the area by the two patrol units that were first responding to the silent alarm, and I was arrested in the area, inside the town of Mill Valley, about an hour later.

Although it wasn't a slam dunk case against me, Kit Mitchell was unwilling to deal with me on any kind of pretrial deal of a reduced sentence for a guilty plea from me. Apparently, she was still way far away from developing anything close to the fantasy I shared about her. Something about that chick. Well, my butt was bound over to Superior court, and next, we would set a date for a jury trial, and Kit stood fast on no pretrial deal. She was hell-bent on sending me up the river of no return, although the ball-busting law called "Three Strikes-You're out" had not come into effect yet. At the time, in the state of California, they did have prior criminal conviction enhancements.

One such enhancement was known as "Proposition Eight," which was a serious felony conviction enhancement. It read: If you were convicted of a serious felony before and you were about to be convicted of another serious felony, you could receive an additional five years on your sentence for every single prior serious felony conviction. My sorry Irish ass had two previous serious felony convictions, which meant I could get two propositions, eight enhancements, and ten years total. That is even before the sentence of the new serious felony is imposed. The new serious felony (the Mill Valley heist) carried a maximum sentence of six years. After doing the math, I was looking at sixteen years in prison, and you could bet Kit wanted to hit me with every minute of it.

CHAPTER 21

Prison Politics

We went round and round between my attorney and the District Attorney's office. We battled for over six months, and what it all finally boiled down to was that the case against me was just circumstantial, and going to trial without solid evidence is what made Kit Mitchell and the District Attorney's office deal with me and my attorney It must have got Kit in quite a twist for I knew she wished for a public stoning. Something about that chick. In return for a guilty plea, I received a sentence of five years for only one proposition eight serious felony enhancement. They dropped the other one.

Plus, I was sentenced to an additional six years for the Mill Valley bungled heist- both sentences to run consecutive, giving me a total of eleven years in prison. Since I had already been in custody for two years, my attorney automatically asked the judge for credit for time already served. Kit Mitchell objected immediately, saying I was in custody on an unrelated case out in Kansas under federal jurisdiction. My attorney countered, citing the fact that the entire time I was in Kansas custody, Marin County had a no bail bold on preventing me from making bail. You may remember I won a decision in the California appellate court on the same issue. The decision that I won was even noted for publication in the California penal law book, "McCarthy vs. California, 1987".

My attorney even reminded the judge of this by citing my own case log. Ol Kit dug in with both high heels; she wasn't about to lose this fight. She went as far back as my juvenile history to try to prove to the judge, in her words, what an evil monster I was. Now, I've been saddled with a lot of names in my life, but "evil monster"? I know I've done some pretty rotten things in my life, but I've never physically hurt anyone with my lifelong stupidity, with the exception of one convicted rapist who also eats his victims. I beat him with a pipe while in San Quentin prison, and I also knocked out the teeth of two child abusers in Tracy prison. I'm not sure if not physically hurting anyone during my crimes will keep me from going to hell, but I sure hope so. I know God won't hold against me beating the hark off two child abusers inside Tracy prison or the coward rapist in San Quentin.

God and I already talked about it all in the confessional. Still, Ol 'Kit called me an evil monster. That didn't sit well with me at all. I believe that anyone who knows me would agree that the word evil does not describe me. After Kit made an impressive speech, the judge sided with him and he told my attorney to pretty much "shut up" and take it up with the appellate courts. That wasn't the end. Two years later, the appellate court sided with me, basing their decision on my own case log: "McCarthy vs. California, credit for time served, 1987". Over the years, I've run into a few convicts who have used my same case log on appeals to win judgments based on credit for time served. I know for sure when my gal Kit heard of my victory she must have boiled like an egg. Something about that chick. Well, I was off to San Quentin again to be evaluated as to where I would serve my eleven-year sentence. San Quentin's entire west block was turned into part of the Northern California Reception Center, where newly convicted arrivals to the prison system were housed. West block had become a complete zoo- screaming and yelling all day and night where a few years earlier, you would have been killed for making such noise. Those days were gone from San Quentin.

Today San Quentin is filled with disrespectful cowards who condone living with snitches, rapists and child abusers. Not that there was really anything to hold your head high about if you were in San Quentin in the first place, but if there ever was, it certainly wasn't now. After a couple of irritating months in Quentin, I was sent to a fairly new prison called Corcoran, located just outside Fresno, California. The prison's landscape reminded me of an ashtray. Its cell blocks and buildings were all pre-fabricated. The concrete walls were poured someplace else and brought here to "Ashtray, California" and assembled together like a large Lego set. The prison had three mainline yards and two lockdown yards. These lockdown yards were called segregated housing units, also nicknamed "The Hole." These two segregated housing unit yards were huge and larger than any hole I'd ever seen. Both of the units were as big as the three mainline yards. Business was good with the California Department of Corrections. These two segregated housing units housed some of the unruliest convicts from all over the prison system. Sirhan-Sirhan called this place home, as did old Charlie Manson. I met Charlie years before inside Vacaville prison.

I actually walked to the prison recreation yard with him one day, and I introduced myself. He would ask me questions from time to time about new cars and movies-nothing special. But one day, I watched Charlie walking the prison yard jogging track, and he was pushing "Daddy long-legged spiders" off the jogging track so they wouldn't be stepped on a true story.

Anyway, here I am, inside Corcoran State Prison, and this place turned out to be a real ball-buster and not because of the class of convicts in residence. What I mean is the prison was classified as high security, and it had all the career criminals you need to fill a prison of that level. It also had plenty of prison gang tension. But the real problem was the friggin' guards! They were fucking out of control! They were putting rival gang members together on the segregated housing unit yards, two on two, and making bets on the outcome of the fights. You are sent to the segregated housing unit yards wearing nothing more than your boxer shorts and shoes. The segregated housing unit yards are all caged in under complete gun coverage. So, your ass is like a gladiator being sent into the coliseum to face battle for Cesar's pleasure.

No shit. This crap went on for years inside Corcoran prison. A couple of convicts were even killed, so shit hit the fan for the guard's hack in the early 1990s. A bunch of the guards were brought up on charges of orchestrating the fights, but naturally, they were all found not guilty. It was all covered by CNN and local news channels. These guard-induced battles inside Corcoran prison walls went on for years. I don't know about anyone else, but me; full-out brawling in my boxer shorts with a dirty cop pointing an automatic rifle at me makes for a nerve-racking rough time! That was not the only problem with the hacks (guards) inside Corcoran. They had a goon squad (special security squad) that traveled around the prison eight to ten members deep, and all wore lead-filled leather gloves, beating the hell out of one or two convicts at a time. They only had one requirement in the goon squad-you had to weigh at least two hundred and eighty pounds.

These fucking cowardly guards would jump a convict by himself, beat him unconscious, and the convict would wake up inside the segregated housing unit. When he healed up, he would then become a part of the betting battles for the guards' entertainment. It was the wild, wild west for these prison guards. Six months into my two-year stay at Corcoran,

I received a letter from a mouth-watering pretty lady that I knew from high school. It was a pleasant surprise since I hadn't heard from Dish in more than a few years. It was nice to correspond with a lady I cared for. It warmed my heart. Her name was Cherry, and we made arrangements to have her come and visit my sorry butt at the prison. No matter how rotten a person has been in life, I truly believe the human spirit needs contact or just the touch of another human spirit. You can't realize such needs until you have been without them.

Anyway, it was great to be with Cherry. She even moved to the town of Fresno, found work as a hairdresser, and visited me on a regular basis. I had even found an avenue to obtain a few extras inside of Corcoran prison. Between hugging and smooching Cherry in the visiting www and smoking marijuana, time at Corcoran went by as best it could, right up until some rat dropped a dime on me about smoking pot all the time. The goon squad dialed me in on their hit list, and what small comforts I was enjoying inside Corcoran came to an end. The serious assholes inside the goon squad were on me vandalizing my cell daily. They were on my every move, but they never did find anything which I'm positive made them hate me even more. They didn't give up, though. They pushed forward with their pursuit to find me dirty. One day, I remember well, they stormed into my cell block about an hour before morning unlock. They came right to my cell and woke me and my cellmate up, screaming at us to get dressed and step out of the cell; we were handcuffed right after we got dressed. Two goons watched us as four other members of the goon squad vandalized our cell.

They unhandcuffed my cellmate and locked him back in the cell. They were taking me with them. My immediate future was in question! Their rat had given them my name about the pot smoking, so the heat from the goons was aimed at me, not my cellmate. I was dragged down to the goon squad offices. They had me stripped butt naked back up against the wall inside their headquarters all the time, a goon squad member screaming at me, one goon in each of my ears and three more goons screaming at me from the front, and two more sitting at a desk. I thought, for sure, at least a severe ass-kicking was moments away. Somehow and I don't have any idea why I thought to myself, "Damn, it's hard acting tough standing here naked like I am." The thought made me somehow crack a smile and just enough to piss the guards off even more. I thought I was done for sure. They started in on me even more than before. Screaming at me, "What the fuck are you smiling about? You blank, blank, blank!" Finally, after them insisting to know, with great enthusiasm, about what I was smiling about, I said to myself, "Fuck it, they're gonna beat my ass anyway. I told them that I had a hard time trying to act tough standing here naked."

As I've learned many times before in my life, God works his miracles in very mysterious ways, especially with me. My comments saved me a serious beating, for sure. The three goons right in front of me turned away quickly, smiling but not laughing yet, and the two goons in my ears yelled at me to get my shit and get the fuck out of there. They didn't have to tell me twice. I grabbed my clothes, made it to the hallway still naked, and put on my clothes. I could hear the goons laughing big time. Not wanting to share any more time with these psychos, I made my way back to the cell. God's help, along with my ridiculous Irish sense of humor, saved my butt that day, but if you do think about it, hell, give it a try, strip down naked, and no matter how hard you try or how you stand, you just can't act tough when you're naked. The goons actually backed up off of me until my time was up at Corcoran prison.

CHAPTER 22

From Lockup to the Fire Line

I was happy to leave Corcoran prison; the guards were dangerous, and the place didn't even have a prison baseball team. I was transferred to a prison up in the Sierra Foothills called Jamestown. This is a beautiful part of California, too, even though I wasn't getting around seeing it much. Cherry had moved back to Marin County, and she lost interest in my incarcerated ass. I understood. It was a frustrating situation, from not being able to be alone together to thoughts of the future together and she had family and friends warning her the whole time she was visiting me that it was a mistake. The last word I received about Cherry was that she hooked up with an ex-convict, a heroin addict who treated her bad. I hope she's ok. To this day, she remains in my prayers. She was a huge ray of sunshine in my life, if only for a short time. If you should read this book, Cherry, I do wish you nothing but warm smiles and if I should run into that coward that treated you had, I shall treat him bad in your honor.

So here I am, sitting in a new prison, and from the first hour at Jamestown prison, I could tell life was going to be much better. You see, Jamestown prison was a step down in the level of security from Corcoran prison, which meant a lot less tension among the convicts. The majority of the mainline population wasn't in for lengthy prison sentences, so most of the convicts were trying to behave enough to make parole. Jamestown prison was the training center for the prison fire camp program. This was my whole plan for coming to Jamestown prison, although my security level did not drop low enough to qualify for a transfer to fire camp. It would be in another year's time if I behaved. The minimum security level is what a convict needs to become eligible for the fire camp program. Even though I wasn't at minimum custody, I was in the right prison for when it did. Prison fire camp was the lowest custody on the California prison system ladder-no lock-up! It was exactly what it sounds like-prison firefighting camp. You were still in the custody of the California Department of Corrections, but you were employed by the California Department of Forestry to go and fight mostly wildland forest fires at an "on call" moment's notice. Cutting fire lines was ball-busting work.

The time passed quickly, and the food was great. And did I mention no lock-up? You also had the opportunity to get into tremendous shape, pretty much whether you wanted to or not, so if I could just stay clear of trouble, I could do my last three years in a spot that presented all kinds of possibilities! I know what you are thinking, but relax, I already thought of it. I still had a year to do inside Jamestown prison before my custody would drop to fire camp level. I got a job as a clerk in the receiving and release building of the prison. This spot worked out great for me. The guard in charge was an old hack I knew from Tracy prison and I was able to work out an avenue of obtaining a few extras via the US mail.

You knew I wasn't just gonna sit on my hands and behave. Besides, it was just pot, and, for the most part, pot is harmless. No one gets stabbed in prison over the pot. It's just not that serious of a product. A year inside Jamestown prison passed without any serious trouble, and I was admitted into the fire prison camp program. The first and only time my prison custody level dropped to the minimum. You were required to pass a battery of physical tests to be cleared for fire camp duty, mainly just to make sure you didn't drop dead from the work you were required to perform. It was pretty hard work. I was sent to a fire camp called Baseline. The baseline fire camp was only about five miles outside the walls of Jamestown prison.

The state of California has about fifty to sixty of these convict labor fire camps both in Northern and Southern California. Life inside Baseline fire camp was damn cool-good food, descent weight pile along with all the extras. It was the summer of 1993, and I was running a chainsaw on the firefighting crew. I loved it. Go to prison and be given a power tool to run through the mountains with. I had two saws to run and to maintain. One was a Husqvarna 266. I ran this saw on an everyday use. The other was a Stihl 084 with a three-foot cutting bar that I would use mostly for falling big trees. It was pretty exciting work at times. I was even flown into fire lines a couple times via helicopter, just like the Huey helicopter type that arrested me in Kansas, minus the fifty-caliber machine gun, of course. In the fire season of 1993, we were on a forest fire in the El Dorado National Forest up above the town of Placerville, California. It had been declared a "campaign fire" by the forest service, which meant it was a large fire. Ten thousand acres had already burned and we had 0% containment.

Fire retardant planes were all over the sky, dropping their payloads as fast as they could. They were nothing short of friggin' heroes. All firemen are studs. I was proud to be a part of it even though I was still a convict. Anyway, this one four-prop retardant plane dropped its load near the head of the fire, and as the pilot was pulling out of his dive, the tail section of his airplane clipped the tops of some trees. The airplane crashed a few miles away from the main fire. A four-prop retardant airplane is the largest of the California Department of Forestry Air fleet. When she crashed, she started a fire of her own. The crew I was on and one other crew from a fire camp named Ben Lomond were re-dispatched to the site of the downed retardant airplane. By the time my crew and the crew from Ben Lomond arrived at the crash site, the fire it had created had grown to about twenty-five acres.

It was two o'clock in the morning, and at seven thousand feet altitude, it was pretty cold even in mid-summer, which was the only good thing about the crash site. The cold air slowed the fire's spread. Both fire crews began cutting a fire line around the entire twenty-five-acre fire. It took us about four hours to complete the fire line. A fire line is where a crew of twelve to fifteen people cuts away the fire's fuel, creating a path up to ten feet wide. The crews cut all the way down to mineral soil to prevent the fire from spreading.

A fire crew has two men out front with chainsaws and a series of hand tools following. Well, we got a line cut around the fire, and the men were spread out along the fire line to keep watch, making sure the fire didn't jump the line.

The morning was approaching, and I could make out bits and pieces of the downed aircraft as it became lighter out. I could also see F.A.A. men and plenty of police and medical personnel swarming around what looked like what was left of the front of the airplane.

I was sitting up above all this action on the side of this mountain with my Department of Forestry captain. His name was Dean Chambers; he was a good ol 'boy, most firemen are, and I said to him, "Come on, Dean, now that it's light out, let's go for a closer look." So, I slung my chainsaw over my shoulder, and my captain and I slowly hiked down the steep as shit mountain slope toward this plane wreck. It was a very eerie experience being right on top of this airplane crash site early in the morning, with small patches of fog all around us, along with a lot of still-burning and smoldering parts of the downed airplane. The impact the plane made on the side of the mountain was spectacular like a comet had fallen from space.

The point of impact was unmistakable, with the half-moon-shaped crater left behind. I looked back up to the sky from which the airplane's last path had traveled. There were dozens of six to seven feet in diameter Sequoia redwood trees just sheared off, marking the plane's final path. The reality of being right there was breathtaking. I still had my chainsaw slung over my shoulder, and my attention was jerked right out of those eerie feelings by an F.A.A. guy with a chest full of badges yelling, "You with the saw! Come here!" I immediately looked at my captain, who was standing right beside me. He said, "Let's go."

CHAPTER 23

The Fall of the Redwood

So, we hiked down to where the swarm of all different types of authorities was gathered around what looked like the front nose of the wrecked airplane. The FA.A. guy who first yelled at me to come down there with my saw hiked out of the gully where the remains of what indeed turned out to be the front nose section of the airplane. He met me and my captain as we got closer. He stopped me and told us why he called us down. He said the pilots' bodies were covered under a pile of tree trunks and branches, and would I be ok with cutting them away so the medical personnel could retrieve the remains? I said yes right away without even thinking. At first, I couldn't see the pilots' bodies; there was still too much debris in the way, plus I really wasn't looking too hard either. As I, with the help of my captain, cleared away the logs and branches I could make out a human o without arms or legs. I said a prayer for the pilot to myself as I slowly continued the work. We were almost finished when I was maneuvering to make a few last cuts with my saw when I lost my footing for a second with the saw idling away in my hand. I caught my balance by accidentally stepping on the deceased pilot's torso, and by nothing more than reflex, I quickly said, "Sorry, Homes. My captain saw what happened as he was removing some branches", and he said, "Did you just call him Homes?" I said it was just a reflex, and besides, my first word was sorry!

Anyway, I honestly did not in a million years mean any disrespect! These two men were nothing short of heroes! It was just a natural reflex from my embarrassing prison upbringing. Luckily, no one else heard me but my captain. We finished what the F.A.A. guy asked of us, but before we hiked out of the mountain peak gully, I asked the E.A.A. guy if he might know the two pilots' names? He told me they were Brad and Skip. "Friggin' heroes is what their names are now," is what I said. It turns out my captain and I weren't done helping these F.A.A. people.

No sooner had we finished cutting away all the logs and debris that covered Brad and Skip that we were asked to come to take a look at where more help was needed further down the gully. The entire fuselage of the airplane had wrapped around a huge Sequoia redwood tree that was at least seven feet in diameter. The tree itself was smoldering at the base underneath the plane's wreckage. The problem was the F.A.A. people wanted to get to the plane's wreckage, inspect it and eventually remove it with good reason. They were fearful the giant redwood tree may fall at any moment. They were asking me can I could remove the tree so they could get to the wreckage. My captain and I both said "Yes" at the same time, but the Husqvarna chainsaw I had with me was too small for a tree that size. It had a two-foot cutting bar on it. I quickly hiked back to our crew truck, where we stored our equipment, and I retrieved a larger saw, a Stihl 094, which had a three-foot cutting bar, perfect for falling trees of this size. Stihl chain saws are the "Harley-Davidson" of the chainsaw world. We have powerful chainsaws! I also grabbed a few tree-falling wedges and a sledgehammer.

I got back in record time-I love falling big trees! Big time! Excitement! My captain and I got together and made our plan for dropping this estimated one-hundred-and-forty-foot-tall redwood. The tree already had a good downhill angle to it, so there was no question which way we were going to drop this monster. When a tree this big has to come down, you oblige it by helping it fall the way it wants to fall; too friggin' dangerous to do anything else. With the fuselage wrapped around the base of this massive tree, that's exactly what my captain and I had to stand on to do our work. Here I am, standing on top of the wreckage of the airplane, making what's called a conventional logger pie cut on the downhill side of this tree. A conventional pie cut is exactly what it sounds like.

A pie shaped hunk of the tree's trunk is cut out of the side of the tree in the direction it was going to fall. My captain and I walked around to the hack of the tree, all the time walking on top of the fuselage of this airplane's wreckage to make our back cut of the tree. First, we had to make sure that everyone was safely out of harm's way because the back cut is the last act of felling a tree, and once a tree starts to fall, not much stops it. Especially one this big. Everyone was clear, so we started the back cur. I nailed the gas trigger on the saw and sunk the cutting blade into the tree. As soon as the blade disappeared deep enough into the back cut, my captain hammered two tree-falling wedges right into the back cut behind the saw's sitting blade to further assist in making the tree fall in the direction we mended it to. I was about halfway through the tree, with my captain manually hammering away at the wedges behind my hack cut. I could feel more authorities' eyes on me than the Kansas helicopter pot arrest. Then, the tree started to move.

I shut the chainsaw's engine and pulled the cutting blade out of the tree. With my captain still hammering away at the wedges, with a quick nod to god, the tree fell perfectly away from the plane's wreckage. I'm positive God digs firemen! After the tree settled way down the mountain's gully and all the F.A.A authorities moved in on the wreckage, my captain and I collected a lot of atta-boys! We were going to start our hike back up the mountain to where the rest of our crew was. The first EA.A. guy we talked to stopped us. I think if I remember right, his name was Tim! Anyway, Tim thanked us big time, took down our names, and thanked us again. As we were hiking back up to the fire line, I felt good.

I left that airplane crash site with a warm feeling in my heart like I somehow helped Brand and Skip. I never knew what they even looked like in life, but I think about them. Death, for me, is both strange and scary with how final it is. I've always paid attention to people's stories of experiencing death in short doses, and what sticks in my mind the mouth is the powerful contentment they feel. Most of these stories always refer to such feelings, giving these near-death stories consistency. I don't think it's a morbid curiosity to have for paying attention to such stories. It actually gives me warmth and hope that the majority of these stories cover the same sort of contentment feelings. I'm a Catholic, and I do believe in God, and I've no doubt he's worked overtime on my sorry ass, but we all face the same fate, and I refuse to believe this is all there is. When I get to heaven (I heard that), when I get to heaven I will be inquiring as to why some real good ones, like Brad and Skip, had to go way too soon. Sorry, back to the story. We returned to Baseline camp about a week later.

After the El Dorado fire was fully contained, my captain, bless his heart, put me in for a six-month time cut on my prison sentence. I still had over two years left to serve, so this would have been amazing. He based the six-month time cut on the strength of the work I did at the plane crash site. It all went through the proper channels at the Department of Corrections in Sacramento, California. My captain even contacted the F.A.A guy, Tim, who wrote a great letter on my behalf. I still have a copy of that letter.

Such time cuts were not unheard of. Everyone who was informed of the details said I would probably get the decision in my favor. But "No" was the answer I received. The reason given was that no rescue occurred, and there was no above-and-beyond action. It wasn't hard to accept the Department of Corrections' decision. Brad and Skip didn't get a time cut either.

I didn't voice that statement about Brad and Skip. I just said it to myself. Well, that first fire season ended, and we would be assigned other projects daily, like widening old fire roads and cutting fire breaks along mountain tops. Back at Camp Baseline, we were partying all the time, smoking pot daily, and drinking smuggled-in bonze. A few weeks after the holidays, around mid-January 1994, we crashed and burned. We had smuggled in a few half gallons of Bacardi rum on an order from a pirate, the booze smuggler. All pirates drink rum. Remember? Anyway, the crew I tan with at the camp all got knocked down drunk! After having a blast playing bumper cars with drunk idiots inside wheelbarrows, we were all rounded up, chained up, and hauled off back to Jamestown prison. Damn, what a monster hangover I had that next day waking up back in prison, sort of remembering the idiots we were the night before was a full two days later before I could think clearly enough to say to myself, "Nothing new, stupid-you've woke up hungover in jail all your I was positively whining about it would change nothing." I went out of the prison's yard and found some familiar hoods, scored some pot, smoked it up, and felt a little better. I had a few laughs with some of them who got busted with me for being drunk at Baseline camp. One of the crew even broke his friggin' arm while we were playing wheelbarrow bumper cars, and he didn't even know it until the next day inside Jamestown prison. Well, anyway, I made some inquiries as to what to expect next for the infraction of being balls out drunk while at Baseline camp.

CHAPTER 24

A Fireman in Chains

I lost thirty days of good time, and I was made eligible to go back to fire camp. I would not be permitted to go back up to Baseline camp, although I was allowed to make inquiries to all other fire camps that may need a chainsaw man. I had got word inside Jamestown prison that my old captain Dean Chambers was mad at my Irish drinking ass, but damn it if Ol' Dino didn't look out for me anyway. He had told a Department of Forestry Fire Chief at a camp called Vallecito that a good chainsaw man eligible for fire camp was waiting to find a home in the fire camp system over at Jamestown prison. Bless Ol 'Dino's heart. Anyway, a crew at this fire camp called Vallecito was indeed in need of a chainsaw man, and my old captain confirmed that I was a good man with a saw, but he also mentioned to keep my Irish ass sober. Damn, I was just trying to have a few laughs. Now get this, a sergeant for the Department of Corrections who works at Vallecito fire camp comes to pick me up at Jamestown prison to transfer me to fire camp. We meet at the receiving and release building inside the prison. He seems like a nice enough guy, but hell, he came to get me out of prison. He could have been Hannibal Lecter, and I wouldn't have cared.

Anyway, it was about an hour's drive to Vallecito fire camp. The camp was located up Highway Forty-Nine by the town of Angels Camp, California, in the California Gold Rush County. As we were driving, we made a little polite small talk. He gave me a quick rundown of what Vallecito camp life is like. He asks where I'm from in the world, and I tell him the San Francisco Bay Area, mostly the North Bay, and he starts talking about San Rafael and other cities in Marin County. I said, "You know the area?" He said, "Yes. I used to live in Marin County when I played for the San Francisco Giants." I said, "What the fuck!" Right away, I looked at the nameplate on his California Department of Corrections uniform, and it read: SGT. Heise. I said, "You're friggin' Bob Heise!" He said, "I know." I said, "Damn! If I didn't watch you play second base my whole time growing up!" He said, "You're a baseball fan?" I said, "I'm a San Francisco Giants fan, and I come from a large baseball family of Giants fans." At this point, Sergeant Bob Heise and I, although on opposite sides of the law, became friends. I told him how I watched his career when he played for the Kansas City Royals when they won the World Series! He said, "Cool!" Bob Heise brought his World Series ring to work one day to show me.

So here I am, getting driven to prison firefighting camp in the California gold rush country by Bob Heise, an old second baseman for my beloved San Francisco Giants. Good or bad, shit happens in my world! For me, life at Vallecito fire camp was the easiest prison time I had ever done. The work, most of the time, was hard, but I would just look at it like another workout on the weight pile. Two of my demo derby wheelbarrow crew members from Baseline camp were also in Vallecito camp. We were up to no good in no time. One hood from our new crew at Vallecito camp was a local boy from the town of Angels Camp just down the road a few miles. His name was Lyle, and we became good friends. His family would come on regular visits, and I met them all when my younger brother John and his wife came to visit me. Old Lyle had a great-looking sister who also became a good friend. Her name was Sarah.

The 1994 fire season was just approaching and all crews at Vallecito were in training practicing fire line cutting. There was even an annual fire line-cutting contest in which fire crews from all over the state would compete. The rules were simple. Each crew was given one hour's time to cut a fire line in a similar terrain. The crew I was on won the contest both years I was there. My Vallecito fire camp captain's name was Bob Mergle, a good man but also a ball buster. I liked fire season for a lot of reasons. We would eat great and we also made a little more money. We got paid one dollar an hour from the minute we left to the fire until the minute we returned. I know that's not much but we were serving prison sentences and, therefore, lucky to get anything. For me, the best part about fire camp was that I was a fireman, and I felt good about it. I didn't care how it came to be. I was into being a fireman. I might have been a damn good one in the free world. I even ran into my old captain, Dean Chambers, on fire out by the town of San Andreas, California, that same fire season.

We were able to have a good laugh about why my Baseline camp crew and I got rolled up and shipped back to prison. Ol 'Dino had got the full story about our wheelbarrow demo derby. I told Dean about how one of the boys from the crew had even broken his arm and was so drunk he didn't know it until the next day when we were back in prison. I thanked him for helping me both with Brad and Skip and also for the good word he put in for me to get to Vallecito camp.

Captain Dean Chambers and I parted friends. The first fire season in Vallecito camp was super busy. We were away from camp, up and down California, working on fires. We were now back in camp, and the holiday season of 1994 was with us. I hadn't heard from Dish in years. The bits and pieces of information I got from friends were that she was still down in Orange County, California, met a guy, and planned to marry him. I was still in love with her, or at least the memory of her, and this news hurt. I stopped asking about her for a while. Things with Lyle's sister kept my interest at the time. She was now coming to visit me and we were sharing a lot of laughs together.

A couple of times, she and I made plans to meet just off the fire camp's property so we could share some time alone together. These hour or so moments of passion were some of the most wild, hottest, mouth-watering sex experiences of my life! I guess it was because we were so pressed for time and the bit of danger that fueled our feelings. I would get back to camp after being with Sarah, and smoke would be coming out of my ears. It would be hours before my toes were uncurled. It didn't hurt that Sarah was a very pretty lady. I think she enjoyed the danger of it all, along with everything else. Anyway, our avenue of obtaining a few extras at Vallecito camp was working great. Some of the local hoods that Lyle knew from the town of Angels' Camp would drive by and drop pot and booze off from time to time at a designated spot just off camp property. The setup was perfect. I was born in the month of February, so on that birthday in 1995, we set up a drop for some rum and pot.

For some reason, the instructions came back to us in camp to have Tyke run out and pick up the goods along with the normal instructions of what time of the night the goods would be dropped off. I thought, "Why the fuck do I have to run out and grab the shit on my birthday?" I made Lyle come clean with the reason. He said his sister wanted to see me on my birthday. That night, an hour after dark, I made the four-mile hike at Olympic speed and found Sarah sitting in a friend's van with nothing on but a jacket! A little nod to God, and it was close to midnight that night before my toes could straighten out again. What a way to do prison time! I swear Vallecito fire camp was like being in a. "Hogan's Heroes" episode. Anyway, Vallecito camp was also where I met up with an old convict I knew from San Quentin prison. His name is Sergio. Sergio was a southern Mexican, which meant he was a Sorano South Sider, a pretty well-respected Mexican prison gang.

Although Sergio was born in Tijuana, Mexico, he grew up in San Diego, California. We weren't real close friends inside Quentin. We just lived on the same tier and said hello to one another in passing, but since Sergio arrived at Vallecito camp, we became good friends mainly because of similar interests in the marijuana business. Sergio was at the tail end of a ten-year prison sentence for possession of a couple hundred pounds of marijuana. Sergio had a family in Mexico that was enlisted in the Mexican Federales that patrolled the Mexican side of the border just below Arizona. We talked a lot about getting together to do some business after we finished our prison sentences. I'm not even out yet and I'm making illegal plans already. Sergio was due for parole one month before me. The next fire season went by, and I was able to save about five thousand dollars from both fire seasons at Vallecito fire camp, and once again, it was parole time for Tyke!

I left the fire camp system in the best physical shape of my life. To this day, I still enjoy telling people I was a fireman, even if it was prison-induced. I didn't care; I had seen firsthand what an out-of-control wildland forest fire can do, and I came away from the whole experience feeling as if I'd helped. It was parole time again. Just like all the times before, it was as if Barbara Eden, in her hot little I Dream of Jeanie outfit, slapped her arms together, gave me a blink of her pretty eyes, and, "poof," I was seventeen years old again. For me, parole was a magical fountain of youth. I was thirty-five years old in 1995, but parole, like it always did, turned my mental capacity into a high school senior, and I went off and running.

On that first day of my newfound youth, Lyle's sister Sarah picked me up at the front gate of Vallecito fire camp, and party was the only plan. I stayed the first night of my freedom in a motel in Angel's Camp, California, and I bounced pretty little Sarah off everything in that motel room until morning. Before the motel with Sarah, we drove back by the fire camp and dropped off some hooch and pot at the old pick-up spot. Hell, I was in the neighborhood. The next morning, I bought a little compact car from a used car lot in Camp with some of my firefighting money. I gave Sarah a goodbye smooch and set sail to see my family. I remember the visit with my family as the greatest time. There were a few new nieces and nephews born into the family since I'd been away, and I had a blast winding them all up.

CHAPTER 25

The Road to San Diego

I spent the next few days getting reacquainted with my family and friends. My best bro Bob, a few years earlier, had begun a motorcycle group before I left for prison. "Rip City Riders" was just a few boys getting together for rides but now had grown to a lot more motorcycle enthusiasts coming together to ride. Great news! Bob started a small group of bikers making annual rides to the city of San Francisco from the North Bay area and nicknamed "The Ride- ripping to the city". My best bro Bob and another gentleman named Joe started the group. I even joined them back on a few rides on my first Harley, my old 1962 Panhead. This was when I wasn't a fugitive or in prison, of course. Today, the group has grown to over two hundred members from the San Francisco Bay area to the beautiful state of Oregon. The crew comes together on all sorts of annual benefits, from raising money for members' and families' medical needs to poker runs, toy runs, and lending support on all sorts of charitable events.

The group has truly grown to a size to be recognized in the West Coast motorcycle world.

I know we've all seen the special police reports and undercover rat cop documentaries stating these poker runs, toy runs, and other charity events are just fronts for criminal cities. They're wrong. All undercover rats, on both sides of the law, will sensationalize the telling of their story to make it all the more cinematic. Never fails. How can giving toys to children during the day be twisted into anything other than just what it is. I'm not saying an organization doesn't have a "hard apple of two". Look at Bernie Madoff or Robert Hanson of the FBI or Vick and O.J. of the N.F.L. The group has me as their "bad apple," but I'm getting better. These undercover documentaries, displayed so vividly through cops' eyes alone, are so lopsided with the hate they have for biker groups. They make me think it's something personal. Maybe they watched their favorite girlfriend ride off on the back of some member's badass Harley and never go over it? Whatever the case may be, I've seen and been a part of motorcycle groups doing a lot of good for a lot of folks, especially The group.

Well, I was now home from my third state prison term, and I hadn't yet found a place to permanently hang my hat. My family and friends offered all kinds of accommodations, but my first couple of months were spent in a series of motels. I'm a pretty horny guy, so I needed a place of my own. I finally rented an apartment on Lincoln Avenue in San Rafael, California, and got this at the tender age of thirty-five years old, the age I first obtained a valid driver's license. I shit you not. I know, what a loser. But that wasn't all: I also put my driver's license to work and landed a job as a tow truck driver. It was a local company based in San Rafael. The name of the company was Redhill Towing. The company had the triple "A" contract for the San Rafael area out to the San Geronimo Valley in western Marin County. Plus, Redhill Towing also had the California Highway Patrol contract for the tow truck freeway service patrol. This free, to the public, freeway service was a state-run program overseen by the California Highway Patrol. Tow trucks would patrol traffic hot spots out on the San Francisco Bay Area's freeways during commuting hours. They would stop for anyone, for any reason, and give assistance for free. The tow truck drivers are paid by the State of California. It was a pretty handy program to have out there on the Bay Area's freeways' hot spots. You may have noticed these tow trucks during the commuting hours. They're all colored white with a yellow and blue freeway service patrol emblem. As I said, Redhill Towing also had the local Triple "A" contract.

For two years, I worked the graveyard shift, and I loved it. The local family that owned the business were damn good people. There was even another ex convict that I knew from prison, working for Redhill Towing. I was paid on commission so my pay varied on how many calls I answered. I truly enjoyed it. People were happy to see you when you showed up, and I was helping folks. One part I didn't really like was the police call. You see, along with the local Triple "A" contract, the UW company also handled local police calls, such as impounding vehicles and towaways. One such police call was pretty wild, and I was also able to help out. I was busy running calls on a Saturday night. Saturdays were always busy, but being busy on the commission pay scale is a good thing. Anyway, my dispatcher comes over the radio and says I've got a San Rafael police call on Francisco Blvd. Right, then I think, "Awe, crap. Anyway, I acknowledged the call and told my dispatcher to go ahead, and I copied the call down."

I made my way down toward the Canal District of San Rafael. I easily found the call's location and came upon three San Rafael police cars surrounding some sort of Chevy. I drove around the cop cars and pulled out in front of the Chevy. The officers, plus two plainclothes cops, had some poor slob handcuffed leaning over the front hood of the Chevy. I threw the tow truck into the park, jumped out of the truck, and walked back to the cops and the Chevy.

I immediately recognize one of the plainclothes cops as my parole officer Richard Guyegos and I quietly to myself, "Fuck me," right when he sees me. He yells out. "Tykel, What's up?" He was actually a good person as far as state parole scars go, He was a kick, the way he was all excited to see me on my job I was. Plus, one of the San Rafael officers on the scene was my old Blind Sgt. Mike Kelly. Kelly starts by saying, "Tyke, how the hell are ya!!" Knowing damn well every single one of those local cops knew how. When, where and what I was doing ever since I got out on parole. It was kind of cool to be next to them and not be in handcuffs. Speaking of which, the poor slob handcuffed and bent over the hood of the Chevy looked up and said, "Tyke, what's up homie" My mom got a big kick out of this story. Anyway, I was able to get a hold of the poor slob's sister, and she was able to pick up the Chevy. Even though the tow truck job was something I half-assed enjoyed, it didn't pay enough. It covered my bills, but that wasn't enough for my stupid ass. I was in need of more income and that had always been a dangerous place for me. So, I contacted my Sorano prison friend Sergio down in San Diego, California.

He told me although his marijuana business was doing well, he could always use some out-of-town help. He told me to show up with some working money, and we'll work something out. I scraped together every penny I could short of committing a felony, and the very next weekend, I drove down to San Diego.

In the San Francisco Bay Area, during the 1990's, there was always a good market for high-grade marijuana. Since all the police raids against the growers up in Humboldt and Mendocino counties, the prices had climbed way up. People were getting tired of paying as much as four hundred dollars per ounce of marijuana. The pot coming out of Mexico, back then, was becoming a much better grade of product. Only one problem with the marijuana coming out of Mexico. It was usually pressed or compacted to make for easier smuggling, and this would always take away from the sale value. Remember I told you back in Kansas that when marketing marijuana, looks are what sells a product? So, I made my fire trip down to San Diego, my first of many, and it was great to see Sergio again. Sergio, for the most part, was a very serious guy, but around me, he had no choice when it came to a few laughs and some partying. I met his wife and his kids and enjoyed a killer Mexican dinner at their home. Afterwards, we got to business.

CHAPTER 26

Risk and Reward

Sergio had been up to his old way of life smuggling pot into the United States in between his job as a local truck driver. He showed me some samples of marijuana that had just come out of Mexico. I liked what I saw, but after Sergio told me the prices, I realized I only had enough cash for about ten pounds of pot. Sergio suggested a lesser grade of marijuana that was priced lower. That way, I could buy more products, but I said, "Bullshit. I still want the best you got." I bought ten pounds of the best quality pot Sergio had, plus Sergio trusted me by giving me ten more to be paid for when I returned. My Irish ass was coming back. I packaged the twenty pounds of pot in vacuum-sealed plastic wrap to hide the smell as best I could and then set sail for the Bay Ares. I drove the nerve-racking eight-hour trip, stopping only once for gas. I bought the twenty pounds from Sergio at four hundred dollars per pound.

When I got to the Bay Area, I sold all twenty pounds to one guy for a thousand dollars a pound, and he wanted more. I cleared twelve thousand dollars on that first deal. I snorted a couple lines of cocaine, filled the gas tank, and headed right back down to San Diego. I paid Sergio off and purchased thirty more pounds of the same product. I had to drive straight to work at the tow truck company. I was fifteen minutes late for work with thirty pounds of marijuana in the trunk of my car parked at my job's parking lot. I jumped in my tow truck and ran calls all night long with a smile on my face and plenty of Starbucks coffee. The next morning, I gave my marijuana buyer a deal on the thirty pounds and walked away with twenty-seven thousand dollars. In two quick trips to San Diego, I made twenty-three thousand dollars. It was "Saturday night, fool!" I bought a cool-looking 1988 Ford T-Bird. My mom and I love T-Birds. I bought a badass 1983 Harley Davidson Shovelhead.

With more money coming in, it always equaled less brain power for me, hence the seventeen-year-old parole age mentality. I was spending money with both hands, and Saturday nights were coming three or four times a week. I was back to partying way too much. On one of those Saturday nights, I got pinched for drunk driving. I lost my driver's license, and as a result, I lost my job as a tow truck driver. No driver's license, no driving job. At the time, my stupid ass didn't mind that much because that just meant more time to run marijuana up from Mexico.

With nothing standing in my way like a legal job, I dove into the marijuana smuggling business with much enthusiasm. We moved our pick-up point out to Arizona to a little town south of Tucson called Sierra Vista. Sierra Vista was about ten miles north of the Mexican border. Sergio had family that was part of the Federal border patrol officers that patrolled along this part of the border. For a little bribe money, we were given a clear path into the United States most of the time. We still had the American authorities to look out for.

We had no bribe connections with the American border patrol. I would fly from San Francisco airport to Tucson, Arizona. Sergio or someone would pick me up, drive the two hours to Sierra Vista, and buy a used car for the trip back to California. I would wait in a mobile home outside the town of Sierra Vista until the marijuana came across the border. Sergio bought this mobile home a couple years hack, and this is where we would wait until we received word that Sergio's crew was coming across. Over these years, I bought at least fifteen used cars in the town of Sierra Vista. Sergio usually took them and either resold them or gave them away. I even sold a couple of them up in the Bay Area, of course, after making the nerve-racking sixteen-hour drive to the Bay Area loaded down with marijuana. Our operation usually ran smoothly. Sergio and I would wait at this same spot for his crew to bring the marijuana across the border.

The spot we would meet at was about two miles from Sergio's mobile home and about a quarter mile from the Mexican border. It was just a speck of dirt pulled out along a dirt road with twelve-foot-high brush all around this area, providing plenty of cover. The meet was always at night, and in this part of the county, it got really friggin' dark at night! Anyway, one night, Sergio and I were waiting for a larger-than-usual load to come across, and his crew was over two hours late. We were about to give up and split when we heard what sounded like firecrackers going off in the direction our guys with the pot should be coming from. Sergio looks at me and asks, "Fireworks?" It was late September, so I said, "I doubt it." Just then, our boys fly into the dim pull-out with their lights out and skidding to a stop.

I could see bullet holes all along the passenger side of the truck. The passenger was bleeding from a bullet hole in his leg. They frantically talked to Sergio in Spanish, and I noticed the driver, who was doing more of the talking, was also bleeding from his shoulder. After about thirty seconds of a wildly excited conversation in Spanish, I didn't get a word of it but knew exactly what was happening. The two Mexican nationals just "poof" disappeared into the twelve-foot-high brush. Sergio and I looked at each other, and without a word, we started grabbing packages of marijuana and throwing them into Sergio's Suburban. We had over found hundred pounds in all. I was shitting big time. We finished throwing the pot in Sergio's Suburban, and I jumped in.

Sergio got behind the wheel, and we left the bullet-riddled pickup right where it skidded to a stop. As we were driving out of the area, Sergio told me that a Federally jeep crashed while chasing our boys on the Mexico side of the border, and after crashing, one of the Mexican Federal border cops jumped out of the crashed jeep and opened up on our boys with an automatic rifle. Those were the fireworks we heard. Sergio said his family connections inside the Mexican border patrol police were not on duty. We were well past Tucson before I could breathe again.

As close as that time was to disaster, it wasn't anything compared to the time Sergio and I entered Mexico to make a large purchase and bring it back across the border ourselves. I knew right away we had come up with a bad idea. The day before this bad idea was to take place, I spent the night at Sergio's house in San Diego and listened to Sergio's wife argue with him all day and night about how stupid our idea was. The whole plan for smuggling this large purchase of marijuana back across the border was my idea, but I didn't know that Sergio and I would be the ones doing it.

Sergio's wife hated the both of us more and more as the day passed. Hell, I was even rooting for her in the argument. It didn't help. She was convinced that we were fucked. The plan on the Mexican side of the border was already in motion so we were committed. Arrangements were already made through Sergio's older brother on the Mexican side of the border. As Sergio's wife continued to make more sense. I liked the plan less and less, but having the mental capacity of a seventeen-year-old and the promise of large amounts of money, I obviously went ahead anyway.

I had heard war stories about poor slobs from California venturing off into Mexico with hopes and dreams of scoring a boatload of marijuana and coming back with the same hopes and dreams of big bucks only to get friggin' pinched below the border and end up spending decades in some third world prison wishing they had never heard of marijuana. But I had Sergio with me, a Mexican national who had family and plenty of connections with the locals and even the Federalists.

We were waiting for the call to come from Sergio's older brother, who was about sixty-five miles below Tijuana. He was supposed to call us when everything was ready and waiting at his house.

As we were waiting at Sergio's house for his brother to call, Sergio hit me with a story about how a group of Mexican police kidnapped him, held him for three days, and beat him hourly until he could arrange to buy his life back. I said, "What the fuck! I thought you had family inside the authorities down there?" He said, "I do inside the federal border patrol, but the Mexican police are in a whole different world." I told him no more stories. Sergio's wife had left the house earlier and said something in Spanish that I'm sure was not "Be careful or anything like that."

The phone rang and we were told to start our drive of fifty to sixty miles below Tijuana. It would take us over an hour's drive. We got to the border and slowly drove past the border booths, entering into Mexico I said. "Viva la Mexico". Sergio gave me a worried look, and the old famous words came back into my thoughts, "Fuck me," is what I mumbled to myself, and I wasn't even in Mexico for more than two miles at the time. The plan we had sounded simple, as they always do. We were to meet up with Sergio's brother. Sergio's brother's name was Jose go figure!

Anyway, Jose is supposed to have all the ends of the deal on his side of the border, just sitting and waiting on Sergio, me, and the money we were bringing to arrive. Sergio and I both had twenty thousand dollars on us. We were supposed to cross the border only after Jose called us and said come across. We are waiting for you. So, Jose called, and we were two miles into Mexico. After the "Fuck me" thoughts left my mind, another wonderful thought came into my mind. I had first met Sergio inside San Quentin prison. He was serving a ten-year sentence for smuggling marijuana into the United States. "Fuck me" became tattooed inside my thoughts that day. We drove through downtown Tijuana. If there is one word that best describes the city of Tijuana, it would be "starving." Sergio and I talked about how ugly the city's conditions were. He told me about a much more beautiful spot further into Mexico. We made it safely to the spot where Jose told us to meet him. It was a dirt house about sixty-five miles below Tijuana.

Right off the bat, there were way too many vehicles out front of the house. Sergio said only a couple of them probably ran. Still, it didn't make me feel any better. It looked like a friggin' bar's parking lot. We agreed to stash most of our money inside Sergio's Suburban. We got out, and I immediately started looking at which way I would run first if shit went hard. We knocked on the front door with two thousand dollars on each of our people. Jose answered the door, and after hellos and introductions to three of Jose's friends, of course, we were told we were going to have to wait. Sergio and Jose argue about this in Spanish for more than an hour. Then Sergio pulls me to the side, and with the first words he spoke to me since we arrived, he says, "Tyke, we shouldn't be here." I didn't say a word, but you know my thoughts, "Fuck me." Another hour went by, and nothing. I was losing weight just sitting there. Another hour, and finally, the clown we were waiting on showed up with four hundred pounds of un-pressed killer marijuana. Things looked good for about ten minutes. The clown, either knowingly or not, doesn't matter; they brought a dozen members of the Mexican police with him. They were all armed with some sort of automatic rifles, and they kicked in every door in the place. These cops were the biggest damn Mexicans I'd ever seen. No shit, there wasn't one of them under six feet or less than two hundred and fifty pounds.

CHAPTER 27

Tijuana Trouble

They had us all face down in the living room of this dirt house, and all I could think about was Sergio's wife going out the front door of their house in San Diego. They handcuffed us all with those plastic zip ties, and I thought they were going to shoot us right there. They were screaming at us in Spanish, and I was not going to be the one is say, "What?" They went through our pockets, stole each of our two thousand dollars, and didn't touch the marijuana. They quickly ransacked the place, breaking everything breakable, all the time yelling what I'm sure were threats of nothing nice in Spanish at us. I had three different Mexican police gun barrels touching my head, during which I thought I was a goner each time. A lot more screaming in Spanish went on with none of us saying a word, and just as fast as they all busted in, they split.

They left us all handcuffed with plastic zip ties face down in the living room. Poor Sergio and Jose were the first to speak, and they went right into a heated argument. So, I said, "Fuck this. I easily wiggled up off the floor and made my way into the kitchen, where I was able to grab a knife from behind my back and cut the plastic zip tie." I went back into the living room where Sergio and Jose were still arguing, I cut everyone's hands loose, but when I went to the clown that brought the marijuana and the Mexican police, I actually felt like sinking the knife in his stomach rather than cutting his zip tie. I didn't do it, though, since it turned out we still needed this clown. I told Sergio, "Argue with Jose over the phone. Let's fucking get out of here!" I went outside to make sure Sergio's Suburban was still in the parking lot.

It was still there, and I went inside the Suburban to grab the thirty-six thousand dollars we had smartly hidden. It was way past time to leave. Sergio did not argue with me. Sergio told Jose thirty-six thousand dollars was all you're getting for the marijuana. He said Tyke and I are getting a discount. The total cost of the marijuana would have been forty-five thousand dollars, Sergio told Jose. In two languages, he had to eat the loss. Jose didn't argue. No more than fifteen minutes after the Mexican police left, so did we.

The plan I came up with for getting the marijuana into the United States was a bit of a Kamikaze mission planned to take place at the actual busy drive-through border crossing from Tijuana, Mexico, into California. I just didn't think Sergio and I would be involved in the plan when I thought of it. This is how we smuggled four hundred pounds of pot into the United States on a bright, sunny afternoon. We were no question off to a bad start, but we were also forced to use the same clown that brought the marijuana and police to Jose's house. We loaded all four hundred pounds into a 1988 Cadillac that wasn't bad-looking.

Sergio and I would follow in the Suburban with the clown driving the Cadillac. We headed north. We were still an hour's drive to the border. We made it to the city of Tijuana, and I could see the border crossing over the long line of traffic as we got closer. We were still right on the bumper of the clown driving the Cadillac. It was slow going because of all the traffic.

As we inched closer, I could see the busy border cops walking around by the border crossing booths. We were still a good quarter mile from the swarm of border cops. I could even see a couple dogs being led around by the leash. Sergio and I started lighting up one marijuana cigarette after another and dropping the lit marijuana cigarettes out the Suburban's windows as we inched in traffic closer to the border booths, all the time staying on the clown's Cadillac bumper.

I must have lit twenty marijuana cigarettes and dropped them onto the street, plus we were also dropping sticky, smelly marijuana buds out the windows. My twisted plan was to get the border drug-sniffing dogs to go crazy behind us. In turn, the border cops' attention goes to where the dogs go, as the clown in the Cadillac, Sergio, and I slip through after flashing proper documentation. We inched closer and closer, and will didn't have the attention of anyone except the clown in front of us. Any second, I was expecting to see the clown just bolt from the Cadillac, abandoning the car and four hundred pounds of marijuana right there in traffic. I ran out of marijuana cigarettes to light, and I dropped all the smelly pot we had out the window. We were five or six cars from the border booths, and I told Sergio I wouldn't have blamed this clown for making a run for it now.

We were three cars from the border booths, and a little nod to God did it. The border drug-sniffing dogs got the scent and, damn it, if they didn't shoot right past the clown as the Cadillac became next in line to the border booth. The dogs pulled their handlers and all available personnel right past us in a big damn hurry. It is friggin' worked perfectly! We were all through the border booth sixty seconds later! As we were picking up speed in Sergio's Suburban, now in the United States, I remember looking back and seeing all the border cops running around in traffic just over the border on the Mexico side. I could feel my hair turning gray that day. I looked up at the California sky and, with another nod to God, said thanks for looking out for me down here! We made it back to Sergio's house in San Diego. Sergio made me promise not to tell his wife what our day had been like, and I swore I wouldn't.

Hell, I didn't even want to talk about it. Mentally I was a wreck, but I loaded up my T-Bird with one hundred and eighty-five pounds of damn good un-pressed marijuana. We gave the clown fifteen pounds apiece for his drive through the border. The poor kid was more of a wreck than I was. An hour and a half earlier, I wanted to sink a kitchen knife in him, and now I was glad I didn't. Anyway, that's not my style. I've got to give the clown credit. He did have the "stones" to stay put in the Caddy until the end. I gave Sergio a hug, and with a suspended driver's license, I pointed the T-Bird north. I drove the exact speed limit the whole way home. I made it home to my apartment at about ten o'clock that night. The marijuana was wrapped well and vacuum-sealed enough for humans not to smell it. My apartment's private parking was well away from foot traffic, so I just dragged my stressed ass up my stairs and made myself a couple of serious rum and cokes. I didn't know it at the time, but that was the last time I would lay my eyes on my friend Sergio.

CHAPTER 28

One Last Crime Wave

About two months after our Mexico adventure, Sergio was arrested for a serious assault on some slob chat insulted his wife. His son, Sergio Jr., told me his father almost killed the slob. After a year in jail fighting the charge, Sergio was sentenced to twenty-five years to life in prison under the three strikes you're out law. It was a damn shame. Some slob with a big mouth ruined my friend Sergio's life. I lived well off the profits of that last marijuana deal for over a year. I was drinking way too much and attending as many motorcycle events as I could. Dish and I were back seeing each other on a regular basis. During my last prison term, inside the fire camp, she had hooked up with a guy down in Orange County, California, and had gotten married. According to her, the marriage was on the rocks.

It broke my heart when I received word that my Dish had married another, but she was a babe, so I wasn't surprised. She was coming up to the Bay Area for visits and staying with me during those years when I wasn't in jail, of course. I would stop and stay with her when I was in and out of San Diego working with Sergio. We would also meet on mini vacations every so often.

One such vacation was the Laughlin, Nevada, motorcycle river run down below Las Vegas. It was the good times, sort of. Dish was back in my life- sort of, and the money from the big Tijuana marijuana deal never seemed to run out sort of. Well, the money from the big Tijuana marijuana deal did run out, and with Sergio hack in prison. I contacted his wife about getting together with Sergio's brother Jose. I was hoping for another load of good Mexican green marijuana. Even with the ugly feelings I had about working with Sergio's brother again, Sergio's wife told me she would ask Sergio about it on her next prison visit. Sergio was doing his twenty-five-year to life sentence at a prison called Calipari, which was a maximum security prison just outside of San Diego. Even though Sergio was doing his sentence close to home and family, Calipari prison was a notorious place, as violent a place as Pelican Bay had become.

These two prisons, at opposite ends of the state, were both war zones for career criminals doing forever sentences. Sergio's wife phoned about two weeks later. His wife told me that Sergio said, "No." Without him there, he didn't want me dealing with his brother by myself. I know Sergio. He was just looking out for me, but I was still disappointed. So, there I was, just about broke with going out and finding an honest job, the furthest thing from my mind. The career criminal in me, who always did the thinking, started to make plans. I was about to begin the final crime wave of my life.

At first, my plans were simple, with low-profile heists that wouldn't attract much attention, but what I didn't know, at the time, was that my old bank robbery partner Foud was about to be paroled from federal prison out in Oklahoma. Ol' Foud, years earlier, had gone on to become a one-man armed robbery machine which included robbing a couple handfuls of banks up and down California. He had received a twenty-year sentence in federal prison for his best effort to imitate John Dillinger. He came damn close. Anyway, my path wouldn't cross with Foud's for a while, but it's coming! I wanted to get away from the North Bay Area because even with the heists I had nothing to do with, I would still receive the blame. I had cops cruising slowly past my apartment every hour. Crooks I knew in the area were getting rousted by the local police and also getting quizzed about my activities.

One local hood that I knew really well got pulled over by the San Rafael police, and all they wanted to talk about was what I was up to. The hood called me right after and told me the whole story. He said, "Shit, Tyke, I even had a gun in the trunk, and all they wanted to talk about was you." After I hung up the phone, I thought to myself, "He probably told those cops something to get them off of him. Either way, I had a lot of local heat from the cops; thus, it was time to take the show on the road for a while." As always, I needed a little traveling money. I started with a little recon and researched down in the South Bay Area since the North Bay was way too hot for me. I made my way to a neighborhood called Hillsborough. There weren't many shacks in this exclusive neck of the woods. The only problem I could make out, aside from getting pinched for what I had in mind, would surely bring a life sentence, that the escape routes were risky. The community of Hillsborough was located between Highways 101 and 280 in the San Francisco South Bay Area.

With only two ways in and two ways out by car, that meant an "on foot" escape. The entire neighborhood was made of a lot of money so it was no surprise when my first recon of the area also turned into my first heist of the area. It was the fall of 1997, and if you were an active criminal anywhere else in the County of San Mateo, California, I know for sure that you got away with whatever heist you were pulling off since I kept every police officer, in the county, busy that entire night! Here's what happened.

During my recon, I found a beautiful three-story renovated Victorian-style estate with all the familiar signs pointing toward the estate saying, "Come get me, Tyke!" So, I drove my T-Bird a few miles away and made quick work of the hike back. I had to get the T-Bird out of the area. The game plan was the same as always, smash and grab. With only two ways in and two ways out both ways would be bottled up with cops quick after any type of alarm going off in this neighborhood. No doubt, police response time. In Hillsborough, it is bound to be a little quicker than most areas. I made my way back to the Victorian. The place was truly gorgeous. It had a magnificent front porch running around the place. The garage was separate from the house. The front part of the estate was way too exposed to the street. I made my way to the side yard and found a perfect point of entry. It was an all-glass door leading into a pantry room.

As I was doing my recon, I saw what looked to be much more than just a window and door alarm system. I reached into my backpack and pulled out a roll of extra wide duct tape.

I taped up the bottom part of the glass door in a kinda spider web fashion. I already had my gloves on so I slipped my ski mask on also because it was felony time again. I had been under the cover of darkness for an hour already. I pulled out my buck knife; all ex-convicts carry a knife and hammered on the duct-taped part of the glass door with the blunt end of my buck knife until the glass cracked. I peeled back the duct tape with parts of the broken glass still stuck to the tape until I had a hole in the glass door big enough to maneuver through. I was in.

I had yet to hear any faint buzzing from the familiar sound that alarm systems usually make when triggered. I thought to myself, "Maybe I entered undetected?" No such luck. I took two steps and 'Blam' there it was- motion detector, very expensive, no time to waste. I made my way up the stairs and into the master bedroom in record time. I couldn't find the jewelry box at first. I looked everywhere, and I was just about to give up and abandon the heist when I caught a glimpse of the side mirror in the master bedroom. It wasn't quite flush with the wall it hung from. It was protruding out about an inch from the wall. I grabbed a hold of one side of the mirror, and it swung open with little effort. Ka-ching! Pay dirt! My pirate ass had found the hidden treasure. No real large precious stones, nothing bigger than a single carat, but a lot of gold.

My sticky fingers helped themselves. I bagged up the entire contents of the mirror cabinet into my back pack. I noticed another type of mirror on the opposite side of the two-sink bathroom. I swung this second mirror cabinet open just like the first one. The man of the house had a nice taste. His side of the bathroom safe held two gold Rolex watches and a few other trinkets that I quickly bagged up. I knew I had pulled way too much time inside. Usual exposure for a heist like this is no more than three minutes tops after setting off the alarm. I had been inside for at least six or seven minutes, and I was still inside.

Again, thoughts of the local police response time in this neighborhood have to be quicker than most. As I made my way to the first floor of this estate, I got my answer. The old familiar sound of a Crown Victoria's four-barrel carburetor kicking in when a police officer stabs the gas pedal with his boot and then, sure enough, the sound of tires screeching to a stop out front. I made my way back to my point of entry. Another sound of a Crown Victoria's four-barrel carburetor kicking in was in my ears and, again, tires skidding to a stop out front.

As I wiggled back out through the broken glass door. I had gained entry through my rather larger backpack, full of jewelry, gut hooked up on some of the glass still attached to the door. I had no time at all to be delicate. I yanked on the hooked-up backpack, causing more glass to break away from the door and shatter onto the ground. The noise it made was heart-stopping and no doubt alerting the Crown Victoria operators that this was no false alarm. I was still only in the side yard with a seven-foot high wooden fence separating me from the back yard. I made very short work of getting over the wooden fence. As I was falling to the other side of the fence, I heard, "Freeze!"

CHAPTER 29

The Great Escape

There's nothing quite like the word "Freeze" coming from an excited police officer pointing a pistol at you to make a career criminal run like the wind. I almost went through the next fence. The places in the town of Hillsborough were all huge estates. Each one had several acres of property attached to them. During my recon, I mapped out a couple of escape routes. I hit another fence, and I found myself in the front yard of an estate directly behind the one I had just robbed. Just one block over, I could hear the police radios of the pursuing officers coming up from behind me, and sure enough, another sound of a Crown Victoria's four-barrel carburetor kicking in, coming right towards me and skidding to a stop right in front of my escape path.

No doubt they were getting instructions from my cop pursuers via cop radio. I could hear the two police officers coming up fast behind me. The newest Crown Victoria to show up had not made me move, for I was still in the shadows.

I was in a tight spot, for sure. Cops in front of me, cops coming up fast behind me, and, no doubt, more cops on the way. Some serious ass-hauling was required! No joke! With a backpack full of gold and jewels, my Irish Leprechaun ass got into a panic mode. I darted out right in front of the newest Crown Victoria, which had just skidded to a stop. I don't think he saw me until I was right in front of him. I still had my ski mask on, so I didn't care what he saw. By the time he pulled his ass out of his patrol car, he had no say in the race anyway.

I was blindly flying over so many fences, distancing myself from the first two police officers. I can't believe I didn't get hurt and then I heard it-a helicopter. Western Kansas came into my thoughts. I was hearing Crown Victoria's all over the area and sirens in the distance, but the helicopter was now circling. I knew these city helicopters had all the latest heat-seeking equipment they needed. I had temporarily given the foot pursuit officers the slip, but I could hear them in the not-so-far-off distance, with more sirens nearing in my ears. I could tell the helicopter had not yet made me because it was still circling, but I also knew the helicopter wasn't reporting the local traffic. He was hunting for me. I had to disappear fast. I was laying low, catching my breath, knowing I had to go fast and far to get out of helicopter range. I looked from where I was standing. Next to some trees was a small creek running out to the curb of the street, and the water was trickling into a grated sewer drain. I walked out slowly from the cover of the trees, looking up and down the street. I bent down to get a closer look through the grated sewer drain. It looked big enough for me to fit inside.

With no time and all my prison weight pile strength, I tried to lift the cast iron grate that covered this sewer. At first, it didn't budge, but with the sound of nearing sirens for motivation, I tried again with everything I had and got one side to come up. I moved around to the one side that lifted up and worked the entire grate up from there. I slid the grate to the side of the hole. It covered just enough to fit my butt inside. I maneuvered the grate back into its original position over me using my shoulders, back, and legs. I backed down into one of the sewers' culverts about five feet down. Within a few seconds, I was soaking wet, but my adrenaline was still running hard, which kept me warm for a little while anyway. I could hear all the commotion going on up above me throughout the neighborhood. Police cars were racing up and down the streets. A couple times I even had officers just above me on foot. They didn't sound happy. The sound of the helicopter circling above did not go away for over an hour. It was well after midnight before I emerged from the Hillsborough sewer system. I was friggin' numb to the bone and still soaking wet. I ducked back up by the trees and little creek I'd hidden by earlier. The neighborhood was eerily quiet. I stretched and got a little feeling back into my legs and then started out on the four or five miles it would take to get back to my T-Bird. I had parked the Ford in a little strip mall parking lot, knowing I would be on foot for most of the heist. I made it back to my car undetected. I very nervously started the car and drove out of the area a little before two am.

The score from this Hillsborough heist was large but not as large as the owners of the estate reported to the authorities and, in turn, claimed to their insurance company even close. I cleared a little over twenty-five thousand dollars, and that put the entire heist at a little under one hundred thousand dollars. This was good, especially with no stones larger than a single carat, and the Rolex watches were "low budget" at maybe three to four thousand apiece retail. The owners' claim to the authorities was over five hundred thousand dollars. This was confirmed by the rather large article in the next day's edition of the San Mateo Times newspaper. It was a pretty dramatic article detailing the night's events. The problem with publicity like that is pressure from the law gets stepped up a notch. Also, any insurance company I've ever heard of just does not simply write out a half-million-dollar check without doing some investigating of their own.

I've had some previous experience with these types of authorities. Insurance investigators' usual procedure is to copy or piggyback what the police are doing when they have no solid leads, although they probably had a vague physical description of me. What they would first do is see what local hoods were at large during the time of the heist that also fit the physical description and have done similar crimes in their past. Although I had a similar background, San Mateo County was out of my stomping ground. I no doubt caused a lot of heat for a few local San Mateo crooks that fit a few of the details the investigator had to go on. I would just lay low for a month or so after this heist. There I go again, stimulating the local economy and giving job security to all sorts of employees. I know, I know, I'm an idiot.

Anyway, the twenty-five thousand enabled my butt to lay low for a couple of months. I skipped town the day after I fenced the loot to my wise guy connection. I headed south to spend time with Dish. We went down to San Diego, checked into a beautiful hotel, and spent a few days living on room service and running around partying in the Gas Lamp District of downtown San Diego. The Gas Lamp District is super cool, with lots of nightclubs and fun restaurants. Dish was in the interior decorating business and had just finished work on a home in a very exclusive neighborhood close to San Diego.

The owners of the home were throwing a party, and Dish wanted to go. Off we went to an absolutely mouth-watering neighborhood called Rancho Santa Fe. As soon as we entered the area, my criminal blood started to bubble. This area was way too friggin' juicy and far enough away from anyone who carried a badge that knew my name. Dish would of beat me with a baseball bat had she known what was going through my mind at the time. We had a great time at the party. Dish showed me all the work she had done on the inside of the estate. She really did have a great touch with decorating. Most of what she showed me, I didn't have a clue as to what went with what or even what "it" was, but I liked what I was looking at.

Dish always said she was a pro at spending other people's money. Well, a few days later, Dish had to get back to her career and stop with all the teenage partying I always managed to bring us back to. I had planned a little recon of Rancho Santa Fe before I left town. Dish and I said our goodbyes, and she headed north to Orange County. I, on the other hand, headed east for a little recon and research. I had made a few mental notes the night Dish and I attended the party. I had a descent out of the way place to park my T-Bird, but it was going to be a long hike into the hills to do my recon. I stopped for supplies: a twelve-pack of Coors Light, chips, and candy.

I drove to the out-of-the-way place to park. I got my backpack out of the trunk that contained my complete larceny kit: binoculars, gloves, mask, duct tape, and a few other necessities. I stuffed my supplies into the larceny kit and headed out on what looked like a well-used hiking trail. Up and over a couple of good-sized hills, I found myself amongst the beautiful rolling hills of Rancho Santa Fe. It was still only about four thirty in the afternoon, with way too much daylight to get up close. I made camp with my Coors and candy. I surveyed what areas I could see through my binoculars, and I found a few decent approach routes. It was a beautiful Sunday evening at about eighty-five degrees, a typical Southern California evening. Darkness was coming on slowly, and the Coors Light was disappearing rapidly. This is not a good combo for my ass. I always got sloppy when I mixed liquor and larceny, so I stopped drinking and started to slowly move in for a closer look; at least, that was my plan.

CHAPTER 30

Saturday Night Mode

Darkness was upon me, and the first place I approached was an unbelievable estate with horse stables in the back and a swimming pool that looked like a lagoon in Jamaica. The estate was breathtaking. It also had outside light sensors hanging from the roof's eves, and I could see through my binoculars that these light sensors were all around the estate. This meant if I approached too close, my movements set off the sensors, and in turn, flood lights would surely light up the hillside, so I kept my distance. I was getting a good look at the property through my binoculars at a distance of about fifty yards. I was right in the middle of admiring this place when I heard laughing and cars speeding up the long private driveway. There were three cars. Two convertibles of some sort and a B.M.W. filled with what looked like teenagers and early twenty-year-olds. They were screaming and laughing as their cars came to quick stops out in front of their badass estate.

The cars were filled with five to six kids in each. They all piled up to the front door, where one of the boys was fumbling with the door's lock. I moved in for a closer look. The outside flood lights sprang on as soon as the three carloads of kids came to a quick stop in front of the place, so by staying in the shadows, I was able to get much closer. The boy who was fumbling with the lock Hung open the door and all the kids burst into the place. I made my way to an angle on one side of the estate where I could easily see inside. The whole bottom floor of the estate, on both sides and back, was mostly made of large, floor-to-ceiling glass windows. Most of the kids were making their way to the backyard pool area. I could still see the young boy who was first to the front door. His back was to me, but I could see him clearly through my binoculars. He seemed to finish what he was doing and stepped to one side and I saw it! It was just a half second, but I know what I saw. The kid had just punched in the alarm code on the alarm panel. I caught a glimpse of the alarm panel itself when the kid had finished punching in the code and stepped to one side while closing some type of cabinet door on the alarm panel.

The alarm was off. By this time, music was blasting, and a few kids were already in the pool. At first, the kids were all over the estate, but a little less than an hour into the party, they were all out by the pool and back patio. Even though I was only supposed to be on a recon and research mission, this was way too good of an opportunity to pass on. Besides, if I were to set off any alarms in this area, with my usual method of a mash and grab, I would need a helicopter of my own to escape.

I moved towards the front door, past the two convertibles and the B.M.W. Both convertibles had their car keys dangling from their ignitions - good to know in case things go sour and I'm seen. I could use one of the convertibles to get my uninvited butt out of the area. I try the front door handle and unlocked is how I find it. I crack the front door just a bit and listen. I peek inside and see no one. With gloves and a ski mask already on, I slide in and am greeted by the beautiful wooden staircase, one on each side of the front entrance. I waste no time climbing the staircase on the left side. I was on the staircase no more than two full seconds making my way to what seemed like the master bedroom entrance at the back part of the estate. This place was friggin' breathtaking. As I took my final steps into the master bedroom, I actually had to stop and take a couple of seconds to just look. Unbelievably, the bedroom had an all-white baby grand piano right next to a bed built for twenty.

The jewelry box, tucked into the back of the walk-in closet, was the size of a stand-up dresser. It was the biggest damn jewelry box I'd ever seen. Everything in the place was large. It took me only a minute or so to bag up the precious metals. I didn't notice any large stones, though. A few nice-sized emeralds and a lot of gold. If all was stamped at least 14K then I was in for a nice paycheck. It was time to go. I had a good long run ahead of me, and I didn't need a helicopter over me during it all. If an alarm went off in this area, I'm positive the cops would respond with great enthusiasm. I put everything back as I found it- minus the jewelry, of course. I closed the dresser-sized jewelry box and made my way back down the stairs, and out the front doors, I'd entered through. There were way too many people here to do any more snooping around.

I started off on a light jog back to my T-Bird jingling all the way. I made good time back to my car. I started her up and quickly got out of the area. I hit a Starbucks coffee shop in Carlsbad, California. I didn't hit it! I just bought a double-depth charged coffee and settled into my T-Bird for the long ride back to Marin County. The next day I cashed in for almost twenty-two thousand dollars with my wise guy fence down in North Beach. He said I was the Irishman that he was happy to see. I was back on Saturday night mode. I was still renting my apartment in San Rafael and bedding down as many young ladies as I could. But now I was drinking just about every day and getting sloppy with being a criminal. I was still driving my T-Bird and riding my Harley on a suspended license, and one night in the North Bay area, I got pinched while riding my Harley in the town of Santa Rosa, California. I remember it well because it was the same night that Princess Diana died in that car accident.

There was a group of about five or six of us all on bikes that night. We were in a bar up in Healdsburg, California, when the news of Princess Diana interrupted the ball game that was on the bar's TV and told of her tragic passing. Damn shame, she was such a babe too! This was also a memorable night for me besides the Princess Diana story and the handcuffs I'll be wearing later on that night. This was also the night I became very attracted to a lady we'll call Reba. Reba, unfortunately for me, was the girlfriend of a motorcycle friend who rode with my crew. Reba's boyfriend was a bit of an idiot, and it was easy for me to feel that I could fall hard for her. It would be years before I could act on my feelings for

Reba. I was still seeing Dish on a regular basis, and Reba belonged to another. Anyway, we were just about to leave the bar, and everybody but me had their bikes started up and ready to hit Highway 101 South. I was taking a couple hits off a doobie as everybody started out towards the freeway. I quickly jumped on my bike and headed for the on-ramp, trying to catch up. I made my way onto the highway, and I could see my bike bro's tail lights down the road a bit. I had the right amount of marijuana in me as I throttled myself into the fast lane and opened my shovel head up. I was flying and feeling great with the California Highway Patrol clocking me at ninety miles per hour on his radar gun. I never even saw the sneaky flat foot parked on the side of the highway disguised by trees.

I was way into the city limits of Santa Rosa, California, before he caught up to me and hit me with his red lights. I was now up in the pack of the rest of my bike bros. We all made small efforts at pulling over to the side. Between everyone scrambling for position, it was obvious that it was me. The cop was red-lighting. He stayed on me like a trailer. For a couple of minutes, I seriously entertained the thought of high-tailing it, but he had my license plate number by now, and felony evasion charges were not what I needed. I shut down my Harley and took the pinch for driving on a suspended license but this flat foot wasn't satisfied with just that. He also hit me with driving under the influence.

This California Highway Patrol officer was all cop! The entire time of arrest, he acted like I was armed. I was taken to Sonoma County jail. Four hours later, I was released on a signed promise to appear in court in three weeks. A few weeks after that, I was sentenced to thirty days in the Sonoma County lock-up and, get this, the Sonoma County lock-up that I had to turn myself into was the same lock-up right next to the Sonoma County Airport and cargo container that Bobby-S and I robbed ten years earlier. Sure enough, when my best bro Bob drove me there so I could turn myself in, that same cargo container was still there. I told Bob the story about me and Bobby-S robbing the container. Bob said, "Stay away from the container Tyke and get the friggin' thirty days done." Throughout my entire life, I always told Bob I should have listened to him more.

CHAPTER 31

The Last Getaway

I spent three weeks in the Sonoma County lock-up and I got one week off for being good. I had brought in some pot, so things went smoothly. I was still renting my apartment in San Rafael, but the Rancho Santa Fe heist money was running low. Being present in a balls-out prison riot is a less dangerous place for me to be in than being broke. Yet. I continued to spend money like a runaway teenager. Not much more time went by before I was planning another recon and research mission. I was thinking about the Hillsborough job I pulled off down in San Mateo County a few months back. Although it was a close call with the local authorities, I did like the disappearing act I pulled off with the help of the sewer system. I was visualizing my butt inside another sewer for half a night, and that isn't a pretty sight. If I was to hit that area again there wasn't much choice. Helicopters get a bead on you with their heat-sensing equipment, and you're cooked. Helicopters were sure to be called in on anything involving a triggered silent alarm in this neighborhood. With all this in mind, my recon and research would include the sewer system. I had thought of using some sort of diversion like I did in the Easy Bay with the bowling ball, but I was out of bowling balls. The recon I was on at that moment was about to turn into a heist.

Reconnaissance missions, more often than not, always seem to turn into heists. I would usually happen across some estate with money written all over it and, once again, all the telltale signs of "No one's here. Rob me!" I always kick myself in the ass when I think about how successful I could have been in teaching people what not to do so as not to attract career criminals to their property, but, once again, this isn't a success story. Anyway, this particular place was a two-story estate with a guest house that could pass for a very expensive track home. It was obviously occupied with all lights on and activity visible through the front windows using my binoculars, but the main residence was silent and dark. The backyard was a problem with a sheer rock wall going straight up for about fifty feet, leaving about one hundred square feet, which seriously limited escape routes.

As I continued my recon around the property, I made out the alarm system active as a ticking time bomb. The heist plan was simple. The same as always, smash and grab. One problem remained. Before I could commit myself to this heist by setting off the alarm, I had to come up with at least two escape routes. No backyard meant side yard exits only. One side of the estate had a creek bed running through it, and the other side looked to be my best bet, especially with the guest house in the opposite direction of the creek bed. The other side had a small grove of oak trees and brush for cover. I walked through the grove of oak trees and found a street on the other side. I removed another cast iron grate from the top of a sewer entrance and slid it to the side. Would this be my room for the night? I made my way back to the estate through the grove of oak trees.

My presence inside the estate couldn't be more than three to four minutes this time. No matter what happens inside I had to be out by then. I wasn't interested in hearing a herd of Crown Victoria's four-barrel carburetors kicking in again all around me. Surprisingly all went according to plan, but, damn it, if I didn't spend another cold, wet night in the Hillsborough sewer system. The law was everywhere. They responded to the alarm as if it was a terrorist attack.

As I lay, soaking wet, inside that sewer, I heard the sounds of officers on foot, Crown Victorias racing up and down the neighborhood's streets well past midnight, and, sure enough, a helicopter circled over the area for over an hour. As I lay numb to the bone in that sewer, I made myself a promise to leave the town of Hillsborough alone. I. surprisingly, kept that promise. It wasn't because I went straight and stopped committing felonies but because old Foud was paroled out of prison, and we were soon planning another bank robbery, a very, very bad idea. Foud's made parole from a federal prison in Oklahoma. He had finished with a twenty-year sentence that he received for a series of bank robberies all over the Bay area. I really did not want anything to do with another bank robbery.

It drew too much heat from the law, but as time and our planning went by, I got used to the idea. Sooner or later, my dumb ass could get used to anything, I suppose, like those decades behind prison walls. It's amazing what you can get used to, although holding a gun on people was something I would never get used to, but that didn't stop my dumb ass that day. We were driving around Marin County in my T-Bird, discussing our next move. I was still against the whole bank heist idea so we were doing a little recon in the town of Ross, California. This was a very exclusive neighborhood, but in broad daylight, it seemed a bit risky. You could tell my brain-dead ass was working overtime when an exclusive neighborhood of estates seemed more risky than a bank robbery, whether in broad daylight or not.

Here we are cruising around Marin County, two ex-convicts on the hunt, out of money, out of gas, and, in another hour, out of luck. We found ourselves in the Marin County town of Kentfield. This was a very affluent town built around the junior college of Marin. There was a West America bank at the end of a strip mall a few blocks away from the college. Despite every negative feeling I had running through my body, I made final plans for the second armed robbery of my lifetime. There was an alleyway and a few blocks between Foud, waiting in the T-Bird, and the bank itself. The details of why I was now in such a desperate frame of mind to do what most people would consider an act of madness are unimportant. The fact is I did it, got pinched for it, my family suffered for it, and I stayed in prison a long time for it. On September 14, 1998, here's what happened. I stepped out of my Ford T-Bird for the very last time. It was about two thirty in the afternoon. I bent back into the passenger side window of the T-Bird and looked at Foud for the very last time.

I told him, "If I'm being chased by anyone when I come out of that alley into this parking lot, just start the car and try to stay with me as I outrun whoever is chasing me." I said my goodbye, walked through the parking lot into the alley, and traveled a few blocks more until I was standing directly across the street from the bank My backpack in hand with pistol, gloves, and ski mask all inside. I could never tell you how many times, over the next decade, I thought back to this very time and place and could not believe that I crossed the street towards the bank instead of turning around and returning to my T-Bird and Foud with the words, "Fuck that shit" coming out of my mouth. But I did cross that street and marched right up to the front double glass doors of that bank. I got about two steps from the doors, and I pulled down my ski mask from the top of my head to cover my face.

I already had my gloves on, and as I pushed through the doors, I pulled out the pistol I had inside the backpack. What I did not know as I entered the bank after pulling down my ski mask was there was a young lady sitting in her car while waiting on her husband already in the hank. This young lady watched as I made my entrance into the bank and then jumped out of her car and flagged down a passing car-just my luck. These passing police cars would have kept going if this young lady hadn't flagged them down. Poor thing was probably scared to death for her husband's safety. I would have shot myself before anyone else, but at the time, she didn't know that.

While I was inside the bank tellers' cash drawers, unbeknownst to me, there were two police cars in position right outside the front doors of the bank and a lot more on the way. I pulled maybe six or seven minutes inside the bank after I hit every cash drawer, six in all. I knew I had been in the bank way too long, so I put my pistol imide my backpack as I went out the front doors, more than ready to put on a serious display of speed. I was stopped dead in my tracks as soon as I reached daylight. Two squad cars parked sideways right in front of the bank with both officers, guns drawn, in the "blast the bastard when he comes out" position. As I took a step, I got loud and clear directions. "On the ground fucker, or you're done." Luckily, I had put the pistol inside the backpack. If I had come out of the bank with a gun in hand, I'm sure these excited cops could have sent me to the other side. In keeping up with up with every insane thing I did that afternoon I took off running. I'm not sure why they didn't drop me right then, but I'm positive God had something to do with it. Yet another miracle in which I was kept safe. But the chase was on, and these first two officers were in it for the whole race. I ran with every ounce of strength I had and then some more.

Everywhere I ran, more cops were. They had already been on their way for over six minutes, coming from every direction. It was ugly! I even got double-backed and had to run right in between the first two police cars and the bank! I can still remember glancing at the bank windows as I ran by and saw a couple of the bank employees pointing at me as I ran, still wearing a mask and gloves with what were now five officers on foot and on my heels. The foot chase lasted about twenty minutes. It was loud and stopped all life in the area. I made it to the alley that led to the parking lot of the college, where Foud was parked in my T-Bird. As I emerged into the parking lot from the alley with a very excited handful of cops on my tail, Foud and my T-Bird were gone. At this point, that did not matter. I could not have jumped in the T-Bird anyway with all these cops behind me. I would have done nothing but implicate Foud in the heist. I was on my own and running out of room and energy fast. I was cornered at the end of the parking lot, at gunpoint, by cops coming straight at me and the one coming up fast behind me. I was knocked to the ground. I was kicked by five or six different officers. I was handcuffed with three sets of handcuffs and punched and kicked some more, all with my ski mask still on. One officer pulled my ski mask off, and two of the officers said, "Tyke, what the fuck are you doing? I said to myself, "I'm going to jail."

CHAPTER 32

Nine Years to Redemption

I was picked up off the pavement, surrounded by twenty cops, and stuffed into a patrol car. I saw Foud in my T-Bird a couple of streets over, driving away slowly. Foud was not his real name and he was a lifelong friend. Two years after my arrest, Foud would take his own life by jumping off the Golden Gate Bridge. I was booked into Marin County jail for armed bank robbery. I was in a hard way, for I was honestly looking for a spot high enough to jump from. Two days later, the FBI came and took custody of me. They brought me to the federal building in San Francisco. I was indicted in federal court and booked into a federal detention center in Dublin, California. I was arraigned by a federal magistrate for armed bank robbery with no bail.

Marin County didn't let me leave with the F.B.I. without putting a no-bail felony hold on me. No doubt my girl Kit Mitchell was fueled to get the leftovers off my butt that the feds might leave behind. With the "three strikes, you're out law, all the Marin County District Attorney's office needed was just one felony conviction." The federal government had me charged with a bank robbery and the use of a gun in a robbery. Marin County District Attorney had me charged with the same, plus resisting arrest and carrying a gun on school property. I got that charge because I was chased through the junior college parking lot. The resisting arrest or possession of a gun on school property could carry a sentence of up to twenty-five years to life under the three strikes law. From the federal government, I was looking at eight to fourteen years, which wasn't bad but not good either. I was in the most trouble of my life and facing life in jail. It was impossible to deny that I robbed the bank since I was arrested with a ski mask on, carrying a bag of money and a pistol. It would go much worse for me if I were to go to a jury trial and be found guilty.

My lawyer and I were trying to work out the best deal possible. We weren't sure if a deal could be reached, but we were hopeful we could with my guilty plea. After a year and a half, we were able to reach a deal with the federal authorities. Along with a lot of undeserved support from my friends and family, I had hopes of them writing letters to the federal court judge. I didn't know what anyone could do in support of a lifelong idiot like me. I was just hoping the court would see more of me through these letters than just what they were reading about me in police reports. Well, once again, my family's support proved to be the strongest thing I've ever known, and I'll spend the rest of my life making it up to my friends for the love and support they showed on my sentencing day.

I was sentenced to ten years in federal prison of which I would have to serve nine years if I behaved. Thirty of my family members and friends were in the courtroom that early Monday morning. The judge even commented, "How all these people must have better places to be that morning, but yet here they all stand behind you, Mr. McCarthy, all in support of you!" It made me feel both good and sad. In the end, I asked the judge for permission to address everyone who was there for me that day. He agreed, and it tore me up, but I managed to keep it together and thank everyone. When I left that courtroom, I was immediately chained back up and led through the locked-down catacomb hallways of the federal building.

Right then I made myself a promise of no more crime! I've stuck to that promise, although my drinking would continue to haunt me. I'll get into that shortly. My attorney, a damn good man by the name of Ed Swanson, was also another miracle in my life. He managed to persuade the judge to let us plead guilty to resisting arrest and possession of the gun on school property. Those pleas made my butt ineligible for the Marin County District Attorney's office to kick. It turned out to be the saddest, happiest day I ever knew. I was chained up, packaged up, and sent to the federal prison in Colorado. The prison was inside the Florence federal prison complex just south of Colorado Springs city limits. I arrived in Colorado in the spring of 2000. The prison complex had four lock-up facilities. The ADX was nicknamed "the Alcatraz of the Rockies." I never had the pleasure of the accommodation that the ADX had to offer, and I didn't want them either. All that was visible of the infamous ADX was the roof.

The whole place was underground. I never understood the reason for the guard towers surrounding the ADX. The only thing they were guarding were the prairie dogs. Anyway, there was a United States penitentiary at the Florence complex that was as active as the old Tracy prison back in California. If the ADX was the new Alcatraz, then the United States prison at Florence was the new gladiator school. No bullshit! I spent my first two years in the Florence complex. Most of the time was spent on "lockdown" status.

Most convicts housed in this prison were there forever, and stabbing each other was a form of recreation. The next lockdown facility at Florence was the F.C.L.-Federal Correction Institution.

I was transferred there after two years of Colorado's version of gladiator school. The FCI was a little tamer. This lock-up facility also had its wild moments but nothing compared to gladiator school. I spent the next four years at the RCL. There was also a federal prison camp on the grounds of the Florence complex, but I never saw that place. Life at the FCI was not the worst place I'd done prison time. I had a job in the furniture factory and a spot in the outfield on the prison baseball team. I never drank Pruno or smoked any pot while I was inside those Colorado prisons. The only trouble I did manage to get into were a few fist fights that could not be helped and one prison riot that exploded in front of me, and I had to defend myself. The riot occurred inside the prison's gym with an argument over the basketball court and a few minutes later erupted into about ten white convicts fighting with about twenty black convicts. An Aryan Brotherhood member and his big mouth were the main reason we were all trying to kill each other on the basketball court.

Anyway, this same large-mouth Aryan is off to the side of all the fighting, and he decides to throw a metal mop wringer into the middle of the melee, and who does he hit with this friggin' mop wringer? Me! Right on the mouth, and it knocked out my two front teeth. After the fun in the gym, we were all locked up. The Aryan Brotherhood member kept yelling down the tier inside the hole (the jail inside the jail), "Sorry, Tyke." Well, we got back out to the main line of the prison, and about a year later, I was transferred to a prison in Texas called Seagoville. This prison was located about ten miles east of Dallas. Florence prison did not have a dental technician, and Seagoville did. With a little over a year left to serve on my sentence I was transferred to Texas to see about getting my teeth fixed. Texas was hot and humid, but I got my teeth fixed, and I even played a season in the outfield for the Texas prison baseball team.

On December 5, 2006, I was let out of federal prison on a two-day furlough to ride a Greyhound bus to San Francisco, where I was to turn myself in at a federal halfway house. These places are great for those convicts who are through with crime and doing time. You're housed in a hotel setting, usually in a lousy part of town. San Francisco's halfway house was no exception, with the Frisco halfway house being located in the Tenderloin District. This is a really crappy part of town, but I loved it. I was out of prison and taking advantage of the head start the halfway houses are designed to provide. By going to the halfway house, I was let out of prison six months early, so that alone was worth it. I was able to obtain my driver's license social security card, and see my family that I had not seen in almost nine years. The halfway house even allowed the convicts to be employed out in the world. I landed a great job with a Bay Area demolition company. I joined the Laborers' Union, took a bum text with a propane cutting torch, and was hired by the demolition company the next day.

After I left the halfway house, I rented a great apartment in Daly City with a killer view of San Francisco's Sunset district. I had reconnected with Dish, but she was still in her on-again, off-again marriage down in Orange County. But get this: I had also reconnected with a lady I never did stop thinking about while I was away- Reba. She was busy with her life; she had raised two great kids by herself, and she was a successful business owner in Northern Marin County. We got together and had some laughs. We attended a NASCAR race together at Sears Point Raceway, but the night we attended the 4 of July Marin County Fair was the beginning of a relationship that lasted To this day. That first night together was as hot as Laval. It took two days for my toes to uncurl! Although Reba liked seeing me, it was clear that her career was the most important part of her life aside from her children of course.

At first, I was cool with all of it. I hadn't been home yet for too long so taking things slow seemed like a good idea. Hell, I was just happy to be fitting in somewhere in her life, but as always with me, sooner or later, I manage to rub everyone the wrong way-especially when I'm drinking. I believe I pushed the relationship ideas a little too much, and as a result, I pushed Reba away. I told you that night in the Healdsburg bar, the same night as Princess Diana's tragic death, that it would be easy for me to fall hard for Reba, so I hung on to whatever she let me hang on to. My drinking got worse, and I pushed her away further. I was still working for the demolition company and renting my apartment in Daly City. I also bought a new Harley Davidson motorcycle from my bro Bob. It was a rebuilt FX.R. and damn fast. I attended a Christmas toy run on my motorcycle in the North Bay area. It was the holiday season of 2008. I started drinking early that morning, so by the time the ride was winding down that afternoon, I was hammered. I damn near killed myself when

I crashed my motorcycle. I spent two days in the hospital with a concussion that rocked me pretty good.

I spent the next week at some chick's house that I didn't even know. She had taken me from the hospital, and it was six days later before my brain came back to me, and I realized I didn't live with this chick. I walked out of her house and found myself in the town of Petaluma, California. I made my way to the Golden Gate Transit bus stop and took the bus home to my apartment in Daly City. It was by far the strangest week I'd ever lived through. My motorcycle made its way to a friend's house and only had a few scrapes and a broken headlight, but the local authorities charged me with drunk driving. Plus, my federal parole officer wanted a piece of my butt also. I was medically unable to return to work for at least a month. My union representative suggested if I'm having a bit of trouble with booze, why not try a rehab program? I'm not going to be able to go back to work for a month anyway, and the union will cover the cost of the rehab house under my medical insurance. I thought it was a good idea. I'd never been to a rehab program, and I sure couldn't ever remember getting into trouble sober. Plus, I had everyone I know and love mad as hell at me.

Skipping town always seemed like a good idea when I was in these situations. My court date for drunk driving was put off until I returned from the thirty-day rehab program. When I was about a week away from graduating from the rehab program, two federal marshals showed up with parole violation indictments for me. They didn't take me away right then just had me sign the indictment and I was given a court date. Through all this, with the motorcycle accident, rehab program, and court dates with everybody, another miracle came my way. My pal God was up to his old ways.

CHAPTER 33

Walls I Never Wanted to See Again

Reba came back into my life. It made me feel like I could get through the trouble I was facing easily. Even though I was no longer a criminal, I was still facing time in jail. Please don't get me wrong. I do believe that drinking and driving is a serious crime. Reba visited me at the rehab on family day, and I introduced her to everyone as my girl. It felt good to have her back in my life and a grip on my drinking problem. I returned to my apartment in Daly City after graduating from the rehab program. I returned to work with my demolition company.

A couple months later, I was sentenced to six months back at the federal halfway house in San Francisco for my federal parole violation. The drunk driving charge that California still had pending against me ran concurrent to the six months I had to do at the federal halfway house. This was good and bad: good because I was able to continue going to work at the demolition company from the halfway house and bad because I lost Reba during my six-month stay there. I was in need of more of Reba's heart than she was able to give. I do believe that she honestly tried to love me. Things got worse. About two months after leaving the halfway house, I got two messages on my telephone. The messages were from Reba and Bob, and both of the messages told me that my lifelong love, Dish, had died. She had fallen asleep with a cigarette in bed. The news took my breath. I couldn't tell you how many times over the next few months I had to stop and hold on to anything close and take a few minutes to gather myself up with the news about Dish. I had lost a couple of relatives recently, even my favorite aunt, but with Dish's passing, it was clear to me that I had truly reached a time in my life where life takes instead of gives. I was still at the halfway house at the time of the funeral service for Dish, so I could not attend. I don't think I would have managed very well if I did attend. After I left the halfway house, I moved into my brother Jim's condominium. He had moved in with his wife.

Dish's family sent me a DVD of her funeral service. I know I would have never handled Dish's service in person, considering I didn't even handle looking at the disc of the service. I started drinking heavily, and I contacted an old friend of mine and Dish's, who I'd been talking with from time to time since Dish passed. I told her, over the phone, about the video of Dish's funeral. I was pretty upset and, like I said, drinking heavily. Dish and my old friend, her name is Nicki, made plans to meet at a bar in the town of Fairfax, California, so I could pass on the disc of the funeral. I sure couldn't watch it again. I was arrested as I approached the bar for being drunk in public. Hours later, I was released from jail after signing a promise to appear in court in about three weeks. I never made the court date, for three days later, I was at work, and my parole officer called me at lunchtime and told me to be in her office at four o'clock that afternoon. I said, "But." She had hung up.

My federal parole officer was actually a fair and decent lady and not hard on the eyes either, but she had enough of my drinking. I walked into her office at four o'clock that afternoon, and six federal marshals followed me in. I was handcuffed and sentenced in federal court to fourteen months in prison. The sentencing of my stupid ass to fourteen months back in federal prison took place in the same federal courtroom and before the same federal judge and United States attorney that sentenced me to ten years for bank robbery ten years earlier. I was warned and sentenced back to prison. I was chained up once again immediately upon exiting that courtroom. I was led through the same locked-down catacomb of hallways of the S.F. federal building that thirteen years ago I was led through after my bank robbery sentencing when I made myself a promise of no more crime. Remember? I do. I made myself another promise walking through those same hallways, no more booze! I'll always keep the first promise, and now I'll keep this one. I don't want to make any more promises in these friggin' hallways. I'm now seven months into that fourteen-month parole violation, sitting in a cage in a northern California federal prison. I've been attending Alcoholics Anonymous meetings they have here at the prison on a weekly basis. One of the speakers who came into the prison listened to my story and how alcohol was always a part of my lifetime of trouble. At the end of the meeting, he asked me what my thoughts were on all the crime and time behind prison walls. I said, "It was an embarrassing waste of time." The End!

PS. If anyone should pass on this book to my mother, we will no longer be friends. If she reads this, I would not be safe in the A.D.X at the Florence prison complex.

THE ENDING FINAL CHAPTER

RE-INCARCERATION

Fresh out of prison with a new outlook on life! No trouble, no crime.

Paroled to the city of San Francisco to a halfway house down in the Tenderloin district.

Federal halfway houses are always set up in the seedy parts of town. Lots of temptation and criminal activity. I took advantage of it and got a job. The job was for a demolition company, LVI Inc. The headquarters is in New York. I was based out of Hayward, CA.

I rented a one-bedroom apartment in Daly City with a great view of the San Francisco Sunset district. It felt good to be in control of my life again. Once again, it was parole time for Michael Harry, and I was again transformed back into a juvenile deliquiate and nothing on my mind but party time. I was still occasionally driving by jewelry stores and banks that were not on the way home. I couldn't help the temptation to make some plans.

My drinking has always got me into trouble, and that's one thing that did not change. I violated my parole. Being drunk in public will do that. I was sentenced to 14 months by the same Federal Judge and US Attorney that had sentenced me to a ten-year term for armed bank robbery. I was put in a cell in Herlong, close to a town called Susanville. After release, I moved into my brother's place in Novato. He had an empty condo.

Reba and I got reacquainted, and she moved in. Living with Reba is great. We were spending time with family, going on motorcycle rides and events. I had a Street Bob Harley Davidson. It was a fast and a gas to ride. Not the best bike for two. We sold the Street Bob and got a bagger.

Reba was working full time as well as I was. We saved a little money and bought a place of our own. I had rented from my brother Jim for almost 11 years. Life was good. I cut back on the drinking. Reba was doing her thing with the house. I had a place for my bike we had a yard for the dog.

My life of crime is over. I have a wife I love, and she loves me, yea I know another one of those things that make you go hmm.

The motorcycle group that I ride with has one of the largest motorcycle events in Northern California. They do not trust me to do much. I have been a member for over 30 years. I have made lifelong friends who are like family to me. The older I get, the better I know I would sure make a better thief with what I've learned from all my stupid mistakes. That 17-year-old Saturday night guy taught me a lot!!

I live a low-key life. Riding and working on our house. I rebuilt the garage. It still stands to this day. I was building instead of tearing it down. I set up my Iron pile in the backyard on a platform. Lifting weights has always been a part of my life as long as I can remember. That and Baseball.

I was still working for the same demolition company in Gilroy, California. I was with a crew of about 7 laborers we were demolishing the county library for the city of north San Jose. I was cutting metal with a propane gas-fueled cutting torch, and I thought I had a reaction to the galvanized pipe that I was cutting. Not feeling well, I drove home to Sonoma County. Went about my nightly routine, took my granddaughter out for ice cream went home and went to bed..

The next thing I remember is waking up a different person. I had 5 strokes. I had 4 on my left side, which affected my balance and vision. The 5th stroke left me partially paralyzed and with partial loss of use of my left arm.

A lot more than just some might say I deserved it "serves you right," you freaking crook. My vision in my left was fucked up also. I awoke that morning a completely different person. My days were filled with physical therapy at the hospital, but it was obvious my days playing in the outfield were over, and possibly even the ability to navigate a chopper motorcycle down the freeway was in question, and poor Reba gets saddled up with a gimpy old retired crook. Reba was my angel. She was at the hospital every day. She never left my side. She took care of me and came to all my physical therapy appointments. If that was not enough, while I was in the acute physical therapy unit, I became very Ill and had to have surgery. It was my gall bladder. If Wasn't already I bad enough shape, I was dropped off a gurney and damaged my shoulder which I had to have an additional surgery in the coming months. I was finally released to go home after three long month of uncertainty.

Life has changed for me. I have had to learn how to do certain things again. My wife, my family, and my friends have always been there for me, and that holds true. Reba and I are retired and getting used to our new way of life.

I am off parole, and as far as I know, I have no wants or warrants. My wife Reba, can you believe this she threw me an OFF-PAROLE Party. She figured after 40 years, I deserved a party. I still catch myself planning robberies from time to time, old habits, ya know. Reba gets a kick out of helping me with the planning. I do not expect us to act on our plans. Who knows. Bonnie and Clyde, the golden years. We will see, stay tuned.

We better keep an eye on Reba. She gets way too excited about the planning. Frankly, it's got me a little more than just worried.

So here we are in Northern California with our granddaughter, Teeny. We are now Grandma and Grandpa and happily spend as much time as we can with her. Reba's kids are close as well as my family. I think I found my place.

The End

Merry Christmas, Tyke Run.

Florence Colorado Federal Prison Gymnasium

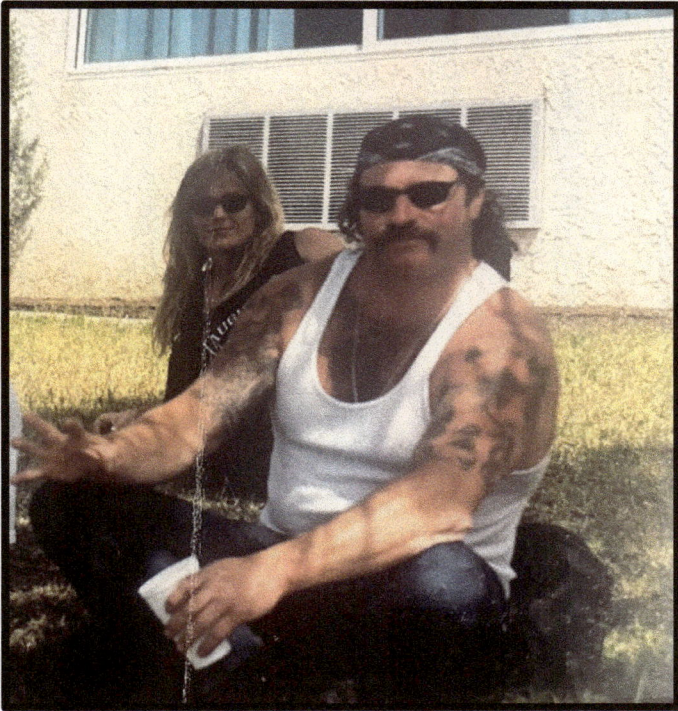

Tyke and Reba Laughlin. NV.

Tyke and his 1974 shovelhead Harley Davidson motorcycle.

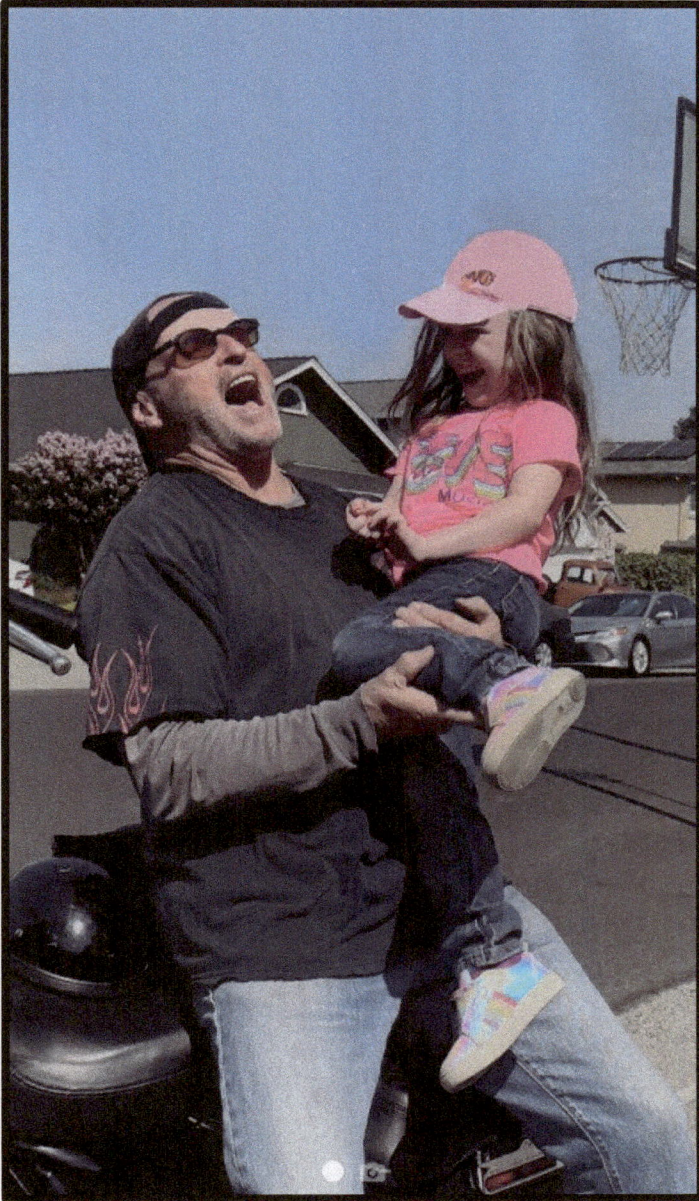

Tyke with his granddaughter "Teeny."

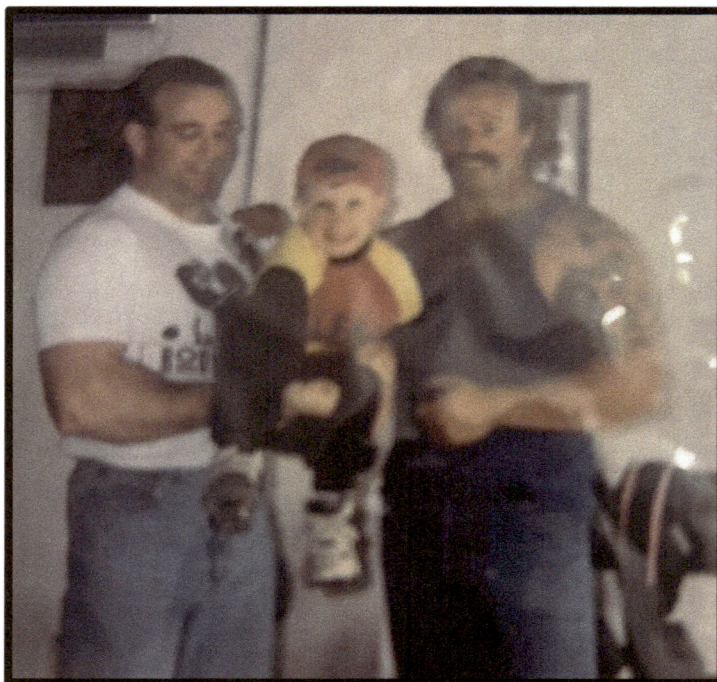

John left, Nick middle, Tyke right.

Our Nephews Police Dog Named After His Uncle Tyke

www.ingramcontent.com/pod-product-compliance
Lightning Source LLC
Chambersburg PA
CBHW052015030426
42335CB00026B/3156